Succulents

for Mediterranean Climate Gardens

Grass-like *Calibanus hookeri* with the pineapple-shaped *Aechmea recurvata* and *Cotyledon oophylla* in flower.

Succulents

for Mediterranean Climate Gardens

Diana Morgan

ROSENBERG

First published in Australia in 2004
by Rosenberg Publishing Pty Ltd
PO Box 6125, Dural Delivery Centre NSW 2158
Phone: 61 2 9654 1502 Fax: 61 2 9654 1338
Email: rosenbergpub@smartchat.net.au
Web: www.rosenbergpub.com.au

National Library of Australia Cataloguing-in-
Publication data:

Morgan, Diana, 1942- .

Succulents for Mediterranean climate gardens.

Bibliography.
Includes index.
ISBN 1 877058 26 2.

1. Succulent plants. I. Title.

635.9525

Cover design by Highway 51 Design Works using author's
photograph of a succulent vista in the Royal Botanic Gardens,
Melbourne, *Agave attenuata* in the foreground against a
flowering aloe.

Set in 10 on 12 point Times New Roman

Printed in Hong Kong through Bookbuilders

10 9 8 7 6 5 4 3 2 1

Soft violet *Echeveria* 'Afterglow': individuals can grow to
40 cm (16 in) across; these all sprouted from a cut stump.

Contents

Crassula muscosa's small, crisp white flowers are set off by dark bracts.

Acknowledgments

I thank members of the Cactus and Succulent Society of Australia for sharing their enthusiasm and knowledge with me.

My thanks to Barry Rasmussen who provided a list of cacti and succulents tolerant of frosty conditions that will be greatly appreciated by those who live in frost zones.

I would like to thank The Gardeners for sharing the beauty they created: Victor and Cristina Aprozeanu, Matthew Brennan and Susan Spencer, Rita Brown, Bert Coppus, Sue and Tony Darvall, Rodney Davidson, Diana Dwyer, Netzia van Eeten, Gordon Laidlaw, Susie Mann, William Martin, Sarah McIntyre, Jimmie Morrison, Bill and Jean Nichol, Barry Rasmussen, Dr Aleck Seltzer, Bev Spiller, Charles and Nola Trethowan.

And the Nurserymen and Explorers for making it all possible: Clive Blazey of The Diggers' Club, Lyle Filippe of Roraima Nurseries, Lara, Jim and Julie Hall from Cactus Corner, Attila Kapitany, Renee O'Connell, Rudolf Schulz, Heinz Staude, Bob Stevenson, Andrew Thompson; and Dick Wright and Renee O'Connell from San Diego, California.

I also thank Wayne S. Meyer, Chief Research Scientist and Business Director, CSIRO Land and Water, for allowing me to quote from his paper 'Water in Australia—where we are and where we're headed', given to the Nursery & Garden Industry Australia National Conference 2003.

John Gough, assisting Melbourne University to establish a School of Water and Land Sustainability.

Michael T. Walker, Gardens Manager, Waddesdon, The Rothschild Collection (The National Trust), for allowing me to reproduce the photographs of the Waddesdon parterres.

Sir Roy Strong for a conversation that inspired.

Dr Christine Ramsay, for sage suggestions.

Stephanie Day of Going Going Green.

Louise Sweetland for welcome advice.

Oliver Frost, especially for help with the names of reassigned plants.

Bev Spiller, a long-time supporter.

The stalwart support of my husband Nigel, the Undergardener, is gratefully acknowledged.

Diana Morgan

Introduction

Many succulents have evolved to grow in low-water regions where other plants fail. They are *clever* plants. They have altered their skin, leaves, roots, their very shapes, to enable them to retain water and reduce its loss. It is no accident that many succulents, large and small, are 'rosette' in shape, which allows precious water to be channelled into the centre of a plant and down to the roots. The leaves of many succulents are round and fat so they can store water in good times, while others have reduced their leaves to spines to lessen evaporation. Some have simplified themselves to mere spheres so that the smallest surface area is exposed to drying winds. Some are corrugated and, depending upon the amount of water available, are able to shrink and expand like an accordion.

Uniquely, succulents metabolise by the form of metabolism known as CAM (crassulacean acid metabolism) and, alone in the plant world, breathe at night when the air is cooler so they will lose the least moisture. The skins of some have a waxy surface to reduce water loss, others grow a powdery covering to deflect the sun. Some are covered in hairs which can capture the smallest amount of mist or dew and slow the speed of winds flowing over the surface in order to reduce evaporation. These fine hairs deflect the sun and the reflected light makes them glitter and shine. Some people think that succulents look elemental and primitive, others think they look modernistic and architectural.

One expects one species to look different from another, but it can come as a surprise to see the huge differences *within* some genera of succulents. For instance, there are euphorbias that look like trees, some that look just like a spiny cactus, and others that are green spheres as round and smooth as tennis balls. There are also cases of parallel evolution amongst succulents, where some species have evolved to look like others in a different genus; for instance, an aloe which can be mistaken for a haworthia, a crassula which looks like a sedum, a kalanchoe which can masquerade as a cotyledon.

With concerns growing about future water supplies, many Australian gardeners foresee a future in which low-water plants will be commonplace, and

Probably *Euphorbia bergeri*, growing in a low tussock about 70 cm (27 in) across. Do not let uncertainty over a name prevent you growing a treasure such as this.

Succulents come in glorious leaf colours: *Senecio serpens*, *Sedum* 'Aurora', *S. mexicanum* and *S. nussbaumerianum.*

plants with high water requirements will be confined to a small section of the garden only, if they are grown at all. They are combining low-water plants from all over the world into a new mix, with few backward looks to cooler and wetter traditions. They are creating intriguing new landscapes using plants that suit their climatic conditions, that are modest in their water needs and are also highly desirable garden plants. Succulents fit that brief perfectly. Surprisingly, because the climate in large parts of the country is perfect for them, Australia is not rich in succulents. A few very interesting ones have been found recently, so recently they have not yet been named but most come from the Central Americas and from southern and eastern parts of Africa.

The Mediterranean climate is defined by heavy rain in autumn and winter, and occasional summer rains which are irregular, violent and poorly absorbed by the vegetation. Summers are otherwise hot and dry, winters mild and frosts rare along the coast, and the light is bright (an essential factor for succulents). There

are several types of Mediterranean climate—semi-arid, subhumid and humid—and local conditions such as altitude can also make a difference. Mediterranean climate regions, with local variations, are found in countries that border the Mediterranean—southern France, the Middle East, North Africa—and the Cape region of Southern Africa, California, Chile, the south-western and southern parts of Australia, even the Scilly Isles and the coasts of Devon and Cornwall in south-west England. All these areas are suitable for xerophytic plants such as succulents.

Wildfire is a hazard in many hot climates, and if it is likely to be a problem it is prudent to plant grass, damp-foliaged plants or succulents near the house as a barrier. Indeed, on a visit to California I was interested to hear that several local councils have brought in a bylaw that any ground left bare when building a house has to be planted with succulents. Succulent trailers such as ice plants and pigface make a very effective fire-retardant groundcover.

Water

Shortage of water is a worldwide concern. In urban Australia 10 per cent of total water use is domestic; each person uses an average of 374 litres of water a day, a large amount of this being for sanitation and of which 30 per cent is used on lawns and gardens. Thirty-eight per cent of water sprayed by the average garden watering system is wasted—it falls on driveways, paths, walls and windows, and runs straight into drains. Local councils are already raising the cost of water to encourage people to use less, and new suburbs are being built where the houses have almost no gardens to avoid the cost of water. It is necessary to store more water per capita in a dry climate than in the United Kingdom, for instance, where rain is regular and recycling is practised.

In Australia we have plundered our rivers for agriculture. We squander underground fossil water on high-water crops such as cotton, rice and sugar, even though we know it may have taken 100 000 years to accumulate. The water table has lowered alarmingly in some areas and risen beneath most of our irrigation areas. A large amount of rain falls in Australia, mainly in Tasmania and the tropical north, but these areas are not near the major centres of population. Seventy-five per cent of all water is used on irrigated crops. It takes 700 litres of water to produce 1 kilogram of millable dry wheat, for example. In the garden and on the farm we have to learn to maximise the amount of water going *through* plants rather than allowing it to evaporate from the soil or from irrigation channels. Fortunately, there is a growing awareness amongst politicians and the general community of the importance of healthy river systems and better water conservation.

It is the worldwide awareness that water shortage is a serious issue that has caused a reassessment of the desirability of low-water plants such as succulents. Succulents are an essential part of the gardening alphabet, and deserve to be better known and more widely used.

My ideal reader

Perhaps you are a farmer and the dams have dried, you're having to truck in water, you are determined to save the cattle, the best rams, and you've decided you have to 'let the garden go'. You're going to miss the roses, and you may not appreciate succulents, but you've *got* to think Less Water. You have selected crops for your particular conditions, but you haven't yet done the same for your garden.

Perhaps you have simply become fascinated with the mechanisms nature adopts to cope with dry conditions. Perhaps you're struggling with a job and children, and a high-maintenance partner, and you want, or need, a low-maintenance town garden. You may want something different to welcome you when you come up the driveway of your holiday house or when you walk into that apartment with its small, hot balcony. You have painted your apartment in vibrant colours, and you need plants to suit, or you like the minimalist look and want one sculptural focal point. Maybe you've got some beautiful pots, which are a nuisance to water, and you want to replace those high-water plants with something less demanding. A succulent would do nicely, but it has to be the right one, and you know nothing about succulents. If you think you don't like succulents, the chances are you may not have seen any that are well grown. Succulents are hard to kill, and that too often means they hang around in neglected gardens looking frightful, which is most probably when you have seen them.

You're my ideal reader! I have tried to write the book I would have liked to have had when I started to garden with succulents

How to begin

A superbly grown succulent from a chic nursery can be expensive, so how do you embark on this new way of gardening without things getting out of hand financially? Study the offerings in the chic nursery, then get the ones you want from a mail order outlet. The plants are smaller, but they are good, and better value. Keep some secateurs, plastic bags, a trowel, in the car. Give a prize to any child who sees a succulent out the window on country drives—this is especially easy in winter when the aloes (red) and aeoniums (yellow) flower. Country rubbish tips are a great source of treasures—there are often beautiful things that have escaped from garden rubbish, rare irises, aloes, and so on. Nurseries tend to carry little variety in the way of succulents unless they are specialists. If you want new plants to multiply, grow them fairly softly (that is, add a little cow manure or fertiliser and water regularly) because succulents grow fast when they are pampered, and by the end of a summer you'll have a good lot to play with.

While this book is about succulents, I'm not trying to convince you to grow only succulents. There are many other wonderful dry-country plants and herbs, as well as beautiful Australian natives, that combine to make gardening in hot climates a joy. All gardens have an overall climate and within them a range of microclimates. Many gardens have a difficult dry area, and the choice of a plant that is a native of a dry area can turn such a place into a thing of beauty. Dry-country plants look comfortable and beautiful in the dry conditions in which they have adapted themselves to thrive.

I have tried to describe the plants in a way that makes it possible for a novice to visualise how they can be used and how they will look in a garden. Succulents are the easiest of all plants to grow, but remember that any group of plants, whatever they are, always looks best if there is a mixture of foliage textures. I take care in my garden to have contrasting leaf shapes and textures. Some of the best contrast plants are bulbs, which is why I have ended each chapter with a companion bulb. Succulents can be mixed in with other plants, and on the hottest and driest day when you may be feeling a little limp they will be looking so perky you'll wonder what all the fuss is about.

There are few common names for succulents. If you are a newcomer to these plants, don't be put off by the botanical names, you'll become used to them. Many species are in the process of being reclassified, but the names given here are as up to date as I can make them. Sometimes succulents that are particularly successful in a certain area have been handed around so many times that their names have been lost. This in no way diminishes their value and I have incorporated examples where appropriate. They are part of a treasure-house of interesting succulents to be explored and enjoyed and which will solve many of your gardening problems at the same time.

I have simplified some names. For instance, where correctly one should write *Aeonium arboreum* 'Zwartkop' (a cultivated variety which can only be perpetuated by vegetative propagation, not by seed), after the first mention the name is shortened to the conversational *Aeonium* 'Zwartkop' (if more than one *Aeonium* is mentioned in sequence, *Aeonium* becomes *A.* var. means the variety, x means a hybrid.

My conversion to succulents

Succulents have not been much grown in Australia for the last hundred years or so. Before that, when stalwart enthusiasts carved gardens out of the bush with only the water they could spare or carry, succulents, many of them brought by the rush of miners from the Californian goldfields, were often their undemanding and yet rewarding mainstays. Later, with water now 'on tap', they were replaced in popular favour by European flowering plants, perhaps planted in nostalgic remembrance of the gardens of the Home Country.

I used to have a high-water garden with many tumbling old-fashioned roses, children and dogs. Life was busy but beautiful. 'Souvenir de la Malmaison', a white Banksia rose, 'Lamarque' and 'Stanwell Perpetual' and self-seeded annuals seemed to froth over everything. There were a few succulents almost forgotten in the mix—an *Aloe melanacantha* var. *erinacea*, whose white teeth glittered nicely when the sun was behind them, a flat puddle of *Echeveria secunda*, cotyledons. It was a garden that required constant care in summer, except for the succulents which just sat and occasionally said 'Ahem!' politely by yellowing their leaves a little to try and catch my attention. I began to resent the temperate plants, including the cheery pots of petunias and pansies, that yelled petulantly for water— twice a day if it was hot.

I had trouble with feeding. Everything in my life seemed to have an insatiable appetite. The baby was a fussy feeder, the two-year-old adored food—which went everywhere but his mouth. *Everyone* wanted to be loved best by the dachshunds, who were fed till they were as round as watermelons. The girls wanted their dinner late after homework, the boys needed theirs early, before tears. I *loved* that time in my life (that time of day was difficult!). My husband worked hard and late. He arrived home one day to unutterable chaos. Asked if he envied a friend of ours who lived an immaculate, unruffled life he responded, 'Oh *no*, imagine how *boring* it would be if you knew what was behind your own front door when you opened it!' There was only one thing to do with such a man, and that was to sit down, share a glass of wine, discuss the day and feed him the good meal he deserved. I was always tired, but whenever I closed my eyes I saw only MOUTHS.

One day a rose looked sick. My garden was amongst several to be opened for the sesquicentenary celebrations of our state. I was thrilled with the honour, and when that rose looked sick, it mattered. I took a branch to the horticultural college. It needed feeding, they said. Perhaps I was more tired than usual, perhaps I walked past the succulents more slowly that day, or perhaps they had said 'Ahem!' a little more yellowly than usual, but I realised quite suddenly what I had been too blind to see—that 'Cinderella' had been playing out before my eyes.

The Open Day came. There were magic moments. The two-year-old had entered into the spirit of things and helped—by pruning the lilies. The visitors were a delight. I loved the lady who, with a finger quivering with emotion, said, 'The most beautiful thing in your garden is *that!*', pointing to the lily-pruner, who looked the picture of infant innocence playing in the sandpit; the ladies I overheard saying, 'I *know* she's a gardener—she must have pruned them [the lilies] for a *reason*'; and the man who told me, 'I would like *my* garden to look like yours, the trouble is *mine* takes so much work.' As the last visitor left, ignoring the wailing mouths all around I seized the flowering pots—the Ugly Sisters—and, with a froth of pretty petals still whirling round their heads, dropped them in the dustbin. The next day Cinderella—*Aloe erinacea*—was led full stage, repotted. She turned green and lived happily ever after. I gave her a cheery wave as I passed, baby on hip, a trail of dogs and children—I was liberated from the water run!

There were no succulents for sale in the nurseries then, so I began collecting them from wherever I could: the roadside, over a fence, someone's grandmother, whoever would swap. Cinderella was joined by Snow White and her Seven Dwarfs and then more. Roses love wind and when a new fence, built a little higher, reduced its effect, many of mine died. There are times when life overtakes a garden, but one day I found I had a quite different garden from the one I thought I had and that, moreover, I relished the excitement, the variety and the difference I saw around me. I fell in love with succulents I knew and ones I didn't. I now have far too many, but that is my pleasure. Succulents are certainly not No Work plants, but they are very patient and wait until I find time for them.

It seems to me that often a gardener's choice of plants is not random, that it can be a commentary about their dreams, a longing for the exotic and for the best of other traditions. Many gardeners born and bred in Australia have beautiful Tuscan- or Provencal-inspired gardens, and use plants that suit Mediterranean climates. But others cling to a more English tradition and plant borders of box (which in a Mediterranean climate needs perpetual prinking if it is not to sport a permanent 5 o'clock shadow) and soft, water-dependent plants that look superb in damper, cooler climates but often look poorly in a hotter one. I remember that my earlier, water-dependent garden used to look really good one year in three. It is entirely understandable if you live in a dry climate that an English-style planting can be an echo of a distant lush country, a dream held since childhood. It can be argued that English gardens encapsulate the best of gardening, but no amount of water will keep alive such plantings in a hot (meaning oven-hot) summer wind which is so drying that more than once I have stood in the middle of my garden and been bombarded by flying potpourri from the roses.

It may not be a coincidence that a great number of people I come across who grow succulents were born in cold climates. Cacti, succulents, hot-climate plants may have become, to them, a way of exploring the parameters of their new world, exciting exotics undreamed of in their cold childhoods. I was born in England and when I was young we travelled a lot. I never seemed to belong anywhere, until I arrived in Australia and began exploring what grew in my new climate. I realised I had a new toy to play with—the sun! I explored old, sun-loving roses bred from Mediterranean or Chinese roses, then succulents. Gradually as their roots went down, I found that mine grew with them, and went deep.

I had a wonderful godmother. She was stone deaf, childless and enormously kind. Communication was hard, and when I visited her she would take me to such places as nearby Sissinghurst, the famous English garden, where conversation was unnecessary. One day, there was great excitement amongst the crowd—caused by a silky starburst of leaves with an exhilarating electric-blue and emerald-green flower spathe, *Puya mirabilis* or *P. alpestris.* In England this was a glasshouse exotic, a scarcely to be dreamed of treasure. Years later I realised that puyas grow easily in a climate that suits them—mine!

A beautiful garden is as much of an achievement

The red flowers of *Cleistocactus strausii* emerge from one side of its columns. In the middle are the corrugated columns of *Cereus peruvianus*, while lower to the ground are the colourful trichocereus cacti that have freely hybridised in Jim Hall's hot garden.

as a beautiful painting. It is a mix of knowledge, vision and courage, and so I have named the gardeners in this book. They are not anonymous and they should be proud of what they have achieved.

My brief was to write about the 100 best succulents to grow in a Mediterranean climate. I have divided the book into categories that suit specific requirements. The ten most highly recommended succulents for each category are listed at the beginning of the chapter, and more are mentioned in the text, both to alert readers to the wide range available and to give alternatives that suit particular conditions or tastes.

I am not a *fanatic* about succulents; I love other plants as well. So why do I grow them? They just look so beautiful with their architectural shapes. They need little water, and they look glorious if I look after them and wonderful if I do not.

1 *Growing Succulents*

Information I wish I'd had when I started growing succulents—it would have saved me both heartache and money.

Five golden rules
* Choose plants that like your conditions
* Garden *with* your climate, not *against* it.
* Grow the best variety of any plant; alternatively, grow the ordinary version *superbly.*
* Grow plants you love, then it is a pleasure, not work, to look after them.
* Water well, but not often.

Growing plants well is a matter of trial and error. It is a matter of observing your plants, trying to understand why they do well or why they fail, and then knowing how to alter the conditions to suit them. And perhaps, ultimately, understanding that if you cannot provide the conditions that your chosen plants will thrive in, you need to change the type of plants you grow.

Succulents are the easiest of all plants to cultivate. They survive almost anything. They are easy to grow well, but sometimes hard to grow *superbly.* Their main requirements are strong light, good drainage and to be kept dry in their dormant period, if they have one. In a Mediterranean climate there is strong light even in semi-shade or shade (succulents will not survive in dark, dank places). Succulents are not only easy to grow, they are forgiving of neglect and absence. Most are easy to transplant, and increase readily.

The following cultivation notes are to help you if you are interested in the finer points of growing them magnificently. I have included information which will be known to the experienced gardener, information which if I had known when I began growing succulents would have saved me much frustration. It has been a long learning curve but one also of great interest and pleasure. I trust this chapter will help the novice avoid the mistakes I initially made.

Succulents can be grown in two ways—hard or soft—for different results.

Growing hard

'Hard' means grown in well-drained, poor soil, with little fertiliser, little water: in other words, trying to mimic the conditions under which many succulents grow in the wild. Plants grown this way will grow slowly, and be drought tolerant. The leaves of some succulents colour spectacularly under poor conditions. However, there is often a small margin between growing a plant *too* hard, when it can look thoroughly sick, and letting it grow slowly and 'stress' magnificently (see Stressing below). If you want to stress a succulent never use a slow-release fertiliser, as it lasts too long in the soil; an organic fertiliser such

Euphorbia pulvinata has numerous branches from the base. In the ground it makes a striking cushion to 1.5 m (5 ft) across. This plant is 40 years old.

as cow manure is preferable as it quite quickly gets used up entirely, leaving the plant with little food unless more is added. Some succulent collectors who like to own a vast number of different plants prefer to keep their treasures deliberately under-fertilised so that they remain dwarfed and do not take up too much room. Indeed, they will even throw out a large specimen if they have a smaller one of the same variety that takes up less space. Other growers enjoy exploring the maximum potential of a plant and try to grow the most magnificent specimens using the soft approach.

Growing soft

'Soft' means grown in well-drained, good soil with carefully applied fertiliser and regular watering. I find that some succulents, echeverias and aeoniums in particular, benefit from a little pampering—they grow faster, look spectacular. Sometimes the best approach is summed up as 'soft when young, hard when old', that is, give a plant optimum conditions when it is small, but once it has grown to maturity, feed and water it less. I have suggested elsewhere that since the same plant can look quite different under different conditions, it can be most rewarding to experiment, and if you have spares, to grow the same plant in various different ways. Fierce arguments can erupt when discussing cultivation with other keen growers— but to my mind no course is either right or wrong as long as your plants look healthy and please you.

Some clustering succulents make beautiful mounds over time. If you intend a plant to remain undisturbed for a few years, it is a good idea to add extra slow-release fertiliser at the initial planting. Then, for the clusterers, each year at the beginning of the growing season make up a mix of a handful of fine soil or potting mix, your fertiliser of choice, and perhaps a pinch of soil wetter. Take a small spoon and, as if you were feeding a baby, spoon the mixture carefully into gaps between plants or lift up an entwined mat of plantlets and spoon some underneath. Sometimes it is possible to gently ease an entire plant out of a pot, tease out the spent soil, put some fresh soil and a little fertiliser in the bottom and replace the plant—which will look totally undisturbed.

Succulents in the ground

Good drainage is essential for success with succulents. If you wish to grow them in the garden this can mean raising the level at planting by adding soil and coarse sand so that the succulent is higher than the surrounding soil in the bed, or building up a rockery with soil in the pockets of the rocks. Humus is important not only to feed plants but to keep the soil open. This prevents water running off and ensures that it will both soak in and be held in the soil to maximise the impact of low rainfall. Great enemies in a long-standing clump of any succulent are weeds such as couch grass or oxalis which, if they invade a group, can be hard to remove, so take care at the initial planting. The cure, always a difficult job, is to dig up the clump, separate and replant.

If you want to establish an extensive succulent bed, and you are not confident that your drainage is good enough, plant temporarily a couple of Australian trees such as tea-trees or small eucalypts in the middle. They will thirstily suck up any water that is available, leaving the earth around the succulents healthily drained. After four years or so, remove the trees (before they get big enough to require council permission), by which time the roots of the succulents, especially if there are some cereus cacti in the planting, will be established sufficiently to suck up any excess of water.

Succulents in pots

In the wild, many succulents grow in soil pockets on cliffs or amongst stones, places where seedlings have been able to obtain some protection. So succulents feel at home in pots which, after all, are much like a crevice—well drained with a small amount of soil. Pots have the advantage in that you can vary the soil, drainage and fertiliser to suit each plant. Remember that if you grow a succulent in a pot you will need to give it more attention than if you grow it in the ground, as it is unable to forage for itself.

One of the benefits of pots is that you can move them about and rearrange them at will, so that if one plant has a period of looking particularly fine it can be put centre stage. If at another season it looks tired, it can be quietly escorted round the corner for a rest. Some succulents, such as hybrid echeverias, euphorbias and kalanchoes, look best grown as individual specimens; others, such as species echeverias, haworthias, aeoniums, sedums and sempervivums, often look better if left undisturbed for years and allowed to grow into a mound. Succulents need to be groomed, but otherwise require much less attention than most plants, and are much less liable to die if they suffer from an unscheduled dry patch or neglect.

Pot size can be important

Succulents have developed to survive in a great range of conditions and it is as well to remember this when

Astrophytum myriostigma, called 'Bishop's Hat' in reference to its mitred shape, is an intriguing member of the cactus family. Because it requires a rest from winter watering it is an excellent pot plant.

choosing a container for a particular plant. Some exist in the wild by absorbing whatever dew they can get, and to do this they have fine shallow roots. If planted into a large deep pot, such plants are not able to take up enough of the moisture held in the soil which can then become sour, and stagnant dampness can rot the roots, leaving the plant looking sickly. Some, such as aloes, have a large root system, and others, such as pachypodiums (small spiky trees from Madagascar) and nolinas (ponytail plants) have long taproots, and should be grown in a tall pot. Agaves and yuccas have short roots and are ideal for container growing.

A bonsai dish can be good for very shallow rooters, but they can be *too* shallow for some plants. Also they dry out fast in hot weather, which can be a nuisance unless you are always around to water.

Never pass up a container because it is too large. If you want to use a beautiful large pot, but feel it holds too much soil for the plants you want to put in it, put hydroponic expanded clay balls, or a few jam jars, even old paint pots (with lids to prevent insects nesting) at the bottom—anything to fill it up—and then put in the potting mix. This prevents soil stagnating, it economises on potting mix and also makes a large pot lighter to move. (For more about pots, see Chapter 12, Mod, Mad and Marvellous.)

Potting and repotting

I like to put a piece of flywire over the hole of a pot to make it difficult for insects to get in. If the roots of the plant to be potted are congested it may be necessary to prune them, tickle them out of their 'pot' shape or tease away old roots, then gently place the plant on top of fresh soil in the pot. Carefully firm soil down the sides, being certain to leave no air gaps which will provide instant nests for insects. The soil should stop at least 1 cm (3/8 in) below the rim to make watering easy. Leave unwatered for a few days so that any broken roots can heal.

Never plant a small new plant of any kind straight into a much larger pot. Instead, pot it on and only when new roots have filled the small pot transfer it to the next size up. Often a plant bought from a nursery is overdue for repotting and can be put in a bigger pot at once. To test, gently tap the plant out of the pot. If you can see many roots like white spaghetti on the surface of the soil, the plant needs a bigger pot. If you cannot see roots, put it back. You will not have disturbed the plant and it will continue growing.

A small *Aloe erinacea* in need of repotting—note the numerous 'pups'.

Some succulents grow fast and it can be useful to have a selection of plastic pots in various sizes for this reason. On the other hand, it may be highly desirable to grow a succulent in a small pot in order to keep it dwarfed, a natural bonsai. I grow an *Aloe plicatilis* this way, keeping it small by leaving it in a medium-sized pot. If I put it in the ground it would grow into a tree and soon tower over me. It still flowers and looks happy … and small.

Not all succulents can be kept small. One of my favourites, a *Kalanchoe beharensis*, started life as a dear little Chihuahua-sized plant, with small, brown, felted leaves. After a while it was plainly unhappy in its tiny pot, some of the leaves began dying back at the tips, so it was time for me to plant it up … every time it complained. It grew past the dachshund stage, past the labrador stage, it became 1.8 m (6 ft) high and top-heavy and beautiful, with great paddle-like leaves. At the St Bernard stage I gave up and planted it out in the garden. It had won.

Prickly and fragile plants

When it comes to repotting or transplanting a prickly plant or a plant with a fragile surface bloom, the first thing is to take care of yourself. In dealing with spiky succulents such as agaves, cacti, dasylirions and especially puyas, protect your eyes—cheap industrial goggles from a hardware store are best, sunglasses are better than nothing. Wear rubber gloves and old smooth clothing, such as a raincoat turned inside out so that it will not catch—have no pride! Take sheets of bubble-pack, even newspaper, wrap them around

the plant, tie lightly with string. This will protect you from prickles and also help prevent damage to the spines themselves, which are often part of the beauty of a succulent plant. It will also help preserve the bloom on the surface of the leaves and keep earth out of the centre of the plant, which can be hard to remove afterwards. It is comparatively easy to turn a plastic pot on its side, when a gentle press will help to loosen the soil around the roots, and the plant will ease out, but if it is grown in the ground or in a terracotta pot, it may be necessary to take a strong knife and cut around the root ball. Tease out some of the soil, taking the opportunity to remove old dead roots and deep-rooted weeds such as oxalis.

As mentioned earlier, when repotting do not water for a few days to allow any broken roots to heal. If the plant is tall—an alluaudia, euphorbia or cactus, for instance—it may be necessary to support it in place with a collar and post until the roots grow sufficiently to anchor it again.

The ornamental root or caudex

Some succulents use their roots to store water, rather like a swollen bulb. The roots of these plants can be highly decorative, and can be shown to best advantage by using a shallowish dish or bowl, and letting the plant sit a little higher out of the soil each time you repot. Eventually you may be rewarded with an exceptional specimen sitting high on a swirl of roots. This of course would never happen in nature.

Unusual variants

Some plants have extraordinary variants, and it is good to be aware that they may need special care. Cristate (crested) forms of echeverias, for example, have aberrant growth along the edges of their leaves, which grow so congested that they ripple like the edge of a conch shell. Cacti also are liable to throw cristate growths. Rain can be caught on these complex growths, so such plants should be given some shelter in wet seasons and should certainly not be watered from above. If you feed them too much the leaves can grow too fast and lose the cresting.

Very black succulents need strong light, as do highly variegated ones. A variegated plant has less of the green chlorophyll that enables a plant to use the sun to turn nutrients into food. I have a beautiful unnamed cotyledon freak that has so much variegation that the 'green' is just a few light grey streaks in an

Echeveria 'Party Dress', a crested Dick Wright hybrid.

The caudex of *Fockea edulis* has been maximised by planting in a shallow bowl, and the tendrils swirled into a turban.

otherwise pure white, waxy leaf. It gives me much pleasure. It grows slowly because it has so little chlorophyll, and sometimes it is hard to know if it is thriving in its slow way, or failing. It lives outside in

Cereus peruvianus: normal growth on left, with a crested form (centre) and monstrous form growing from the same plant.

summer, but it overwinters on a sunny windowsill inside, only because it is soooo special!

Potting mixes

You can use garden soil for potted succulents, but you may need to add coarse river sand or perlite to improve the drainage. Often in a city it is hard to get good soil, and you will need to use a commercial potting mix. Always buy the best. (Compare the cost of a seat at the cinema to a large bag of potting mix if you even *think* of economising.) Even so, commercial potting mixes vary greatly, not only from each other but also from year to year. As I write, the so-called premium mixes seem to contain a high proportion of composted bark, which can dry out quite quickly and become difficult to wet. Perhaps because of this it is suddenly difficult to obtain potting mix that does *not* have water crystals added. Soil-wetting products, either added to the mix when planting or applied as a solution, are said to be helpful, but I have not found them as useful as promised, and water crystals which swell up and retain water are not good for some succulents. It is a good idea to add some coarse sand, garden soil or composted soil improver to a commercial mix to keep it open and help water retention, and also some gentle fertiliser such as cow manure or blood and bone. Certain very fine soils can sift down through the potting mix and form an impervious layer low down in a pot. But you will soon get to know your individual soil.

Some seasoned gardeners have their own recipes for potting mixes, using commercial mix as a base. Barry Rasmussen, Gordon Laidlaw and Matthew Brennan are very knowledgeable collectors and propagators of plants who study their plants' needs. They have kindly shared their recipes with me, and I include them here because it is interesting to read about the favourite recipe of another gardener. It is worth noting that few use commercial mix undiluted by other ingredients. Their recipes seem to contain everything except the Philosopher's Stone! I myself do not like to use vermiculite or perlite, because although both are useful to open up a mixture, they also make it hard to check roots for mealy bug. If a potted plant is grown in the open, it is essential that the mix be porous and free draining to deal with periods of prolonged rain. If a plant is grown under shelter you are in control of the water it receives and the precise drainage of the soil is less important.

There is nothing wrong with using potting mix straight from the packet. One of the experienced growers below said he loved tailoring his potting mixes to each individual plant, but he was not convinced that they ever really noticed the difference!

Note: *1 measure = 1 litre (3/4 pints)*

Barry Rasmussen's easily wettable potting mix
   2.5 measures sandy loam
   2 measures coconut peat (coir/peat moss substitute)
   2 measures normal potting mix
   4 measures coarse river sand
   2 tablespoons (1/8 cup) dolomite
   handful Osmocote (slow-release fertiliser)
   (optional) 1 measure of worm castings

Gordon Laidlaw's cactus mix
   1 measure cow manure
   1 measure coarse sand
   1 measure loam (earth from the garden)
   1/2 measure gravel
   handful limestone (or pulverised mortar from old brickwork) for plants that are heavily spined

Commercial cactus mix is heavy and expensive. To minimise the weight and expense fill the bottom half of a pot with expanded clay balls (hydroponic shops) which will keep the soil open and the pot lighter.

Gordon Laidlaw's lithops mix
   1 measure coarse sand
   1 measure sandy loam
   1 measure peat moss
   1/2 measure gravel to 5 mm (3/16 in) diameter

There is virtually no nutrient in this mix, so water with a weak hydroponic fertiliser or dilute tomato/rose fertiliser. This low-nutrient mix is also suitable for stapeliads.

Gordon Laidlaw's epiphyte mix
   2 measures compost
   1 measure perlite
   1 measure coarse sand
   1/2 measure charcoal

Matthew Brennan's succulent mix
1 measure granitic sand
1 measure red scoria
2 measures composted potting mix

The important element here is the well-composted potting soil, bought from the local council. Matthew finds commercial potting mixes go dry quickly, and the nutrient leaches fast, leaving nothing but woody chips and sandy gravel, resulting in a soil where the water runs off and does not penetrate the root zone. He puts everything through an 8 mm (5/16 in) sieve to eliminate large lumps, which are useless in small pots and can also leave air gaps when stuffing crevices in a rockery.

My rich mix for echeverias
1 measure potting mix
1 handful cow manure
1 handful compost
1 tablespoon (US 2 teaspoons) Osmocote (slow-release fertiliser) if the plant is to stay in the pot a long time

In desperation you can re-use old potting mix, especially if you want a low-nutrient mix. This is not rspecommended, but I have done it. To sterilise old soil, place it in an oven bag, add a couple of spoons of water and prick with a fork (so it will not explode) and microwave. The steam will sterilise it. You can also bake it in the oven. Either way, let it cool, add fertiliser and it is ready for use. Do not take this out of the oven in front of a friend—I once did, and although I explained what I was doing, and although I thought she understood, I caught her looking *sideways* at me shortly after.

Compost
Compost is made when plant material decays with the help of bacteria, worms and other microorganisms to form humus, a valuable organic soil enricher and source of nutrients. It breaks up the soil, enabling air to circulate and water to be retained. It opens up clayey soils and makes sandy soils more water-retentive. The gardening world is divided into those who do and those who do not compost. Traditional compost piles required the piling of vegetable matter, garden and kitchen waste, hedge and lawn clippings, laid down in alternate layers of coarse and fine material. Periodic turning and digging allowed air to assist the breakdown.

However, in a warm climate you can break all the rules. I have a compost bin out of sight by the dustbins at the back of the house. I do not turn or dig, and still have good compost. It is essential to have a compost bin with a lid but no bottom which stands directly on the soil so that earthworms can get in. I put anything vegetable into it, the more varied the mix the better, the odd spadeful of earth and the odd handful of bonemeal as they both speed up the breakdown. After about three months, when I want to use it I lift off the most recent additions which have not had time to rot, and use them to begin the next cycle. Compost made this way can look unattractive and slimy, but fork it into a wheelbarrow and let it stand. Forty-eight hours later when the air has got to it, the rotted matter will be sweet, brown, crumbly and perfect for use. Made this no-work way there may be some stalks visible, but they rot quickly once in the earth. If you need a large amount of compost, buy a compost tumbler, a rotating drum which helps aerate the vegetable matter and accelerates the breakdown so that compost is produced within about six weeks.

If you want to increase the output, ask stallholders at your local market or your greengrocer for some of their waste—cabbage leaves, carrot tops, old fruit, and so on—to add to your compost heap. Do this once a week for a few weeks.

Commercial compost has recently become available at hardware shops and nurseries.

Fertilisers
Any plant grown too fast because of excessive fertilising can become sappy and prone to disease. A plant not given the nutrients to meet its needs will grow badly, if at all. A plant grown in the ground is able to forage for itself, but a container-grown plant is entirely reliant on what it is given.

Fertilisers are either chemical or organic (cow, poultry, sheep) in origin. Chemical fertilisers are quick-acting: they feed the plant, but do not include any humus, and so do not improve the condition of the soil. Their formula is on the packet. Fertilisers formulated for tomatoes and roses are ideal for succulents. The three main ingredients are nitrogen (N), which promotes good leaves; phosphorus (P) for sturdy growth and good roots; and potassium (K) for disease resistance and to promote flowers.

Organic fertilisers contain some humus, and are mostly fast-acting, so they can be used up or leached fairly quickly. Commercial chicken fertiliser such as Dynamic Lifter, which has been heat-treated, is good. Untreated chicken manure, for sale by the roadside, should be avoided as it can contain large amounts of antibiotics which can destroy bacteria present naturally in the soil and lessen its fertility. Pulverised cow manure is perhaps the best fertiliser for succulents as it provides an initial boost but is completely assimilated by the plant, leaving no residue in the soil. This can be a great advantage when growing succulents, as certain types develop dramatic colouring if, once grown, they are deprived of fertiliser.

Most chemical fertilisers are designed in the expectation that a plant will be able to obtain some trace elements from the soil. A plant grown hydroponically has to be fed everything it needs, so if you grow plants such as *Lithops* in a no-nutrient soil mix, a diluted hydroponic fertiliser is the best. They are expensive but economical and have a more complex formulation than 'dry' fertilisers. Resin-coated fertilisers such as Osmocote, which release the fertiliser slowly into the soil, are good, but because of their long-lasting effect a succulent will not 'stress'.

If an exceptionally dry summer is forecast, use only a little fertiliser in spring, as overuse will encourage more growth than a plant will be able to sustain in the dry conditions ahead. Also apply Seasol (a seaweed-based garden treatment)—this acts by thickening the cell walls of a plant; the thickened leaves transpire less, which in turn means that the plant uses less water.

Magnesium is essential for the production of chlorophyll. The leaves of some plants yellow in spring when they race into growth, and a dose of Epsom salts soon turns them green again. Magnesium sulphate, sold as Epsom salts, and obtainable at pharmacies and some large supermarkets, is a very good source of magnesium, as is dolomite which is usually an ingredient in general fertilisers. Magnesium needs to be accompanied by iron, so if yellowness persists, a dose of iron chelates will help the plants to absorb the nutrients they need.

Stressing

This technique can be used by growers to maximise the beauty of certain succulents. It opens a world of fascinating possibilities. 'Stressing' occurs when the appearance of a plant is altered by a change in the optimum conditions for that plant. Cold temperatures, lack of fertiliser, strong sun or excessive dryness can all cause a succulent's leaves to colour beautifully in a way that is not seen under usual conditions. In a similar fashion, the autumn colours of deciduous trees vary according to the conditions faced in a particular season, making the displays in certain years more dramatic than others. Many echeverias change colour from green in summer to a cherry red in the cold. *Echeveria* 'Fire Ball' has shiny flat leaves of a comfortable bronzy green all summer which change to a vivid scarlet in winter. If possible, place a plant such as this so that the sun shines through it from behind, when it will light up as bright as fire. *Echeveria* 'Princess Anne' will change from a very pretty, frilly-edged, soft lettuce green in summer to a mesmerising vision of violet and peach in winter. When the weather warms the extraordinary colour will fade away until the next cold season.

Nutrient levels can change a plant's appearance dramatically. The green leaves of crassulas can turn scarlet if starved. I had fed a faucaria to encourage it to grow quickly to fill a dramatic pot. I was proud of it, with its soft grey-green, lacy intertwine of toothed leaves, until I saw how a friend had grown hers. Given

'Stressing' can make succulents such as this *Crassula anomala* colour dramatically.

no fertiliser, it had developed a strong mauve sheen, except mauve does not adequately describe the mix of subtle pink and blue that melded into the overall mauve. Imagine this colour with the usual shaggy yellow flowers scattered over it—hard to see anything more lovely. Echeverias, faucarias, othonnas, sedums, haworthias and kalanchoes will all stress.

Stressing also occurs naturally in the wild, where certain crassulas can vary from black to scarlet, lilac—every possible colour. The same crassula can look totally different according to the type of rock it is growing on. In cultivation it is a challenge to see what you can get a plant to do. For example, see what happens if you grow it on gravel with a smidgeon of compost, or in scoria with a little cow manure. Some swear by a touch of gypsum. The possibilities are endless, and you verge on becoming an alchemist. Mark on a label the new soil or condition you are trying, and you will be able to repeat or avoid it in future. I put several cuttings of *Graptopetalum paraguayense* in a hanging pot without changing the earth. Whatever was in the soil enabled the plants on one side to grow with a green tinge; those on the other were decidedly blue-grey, a quite stunning accident, and one I would like to repeat. There is endless fun to be had experimenting.

Aspect and microclimates

Aspect can also have an effect. For instance, if a plant is placed to receive morning sun, any dew sitting on it will be dried off much earlier than on one that spends the morning in shade but gets baked in the afternoon. This is a consideration when placing plants such as pachyphytums, with their fat, closely packed little leaves—if they are allowed to skulk in a dank corner with water sitting on their leaves for an excessively long time, they can rot. But there are other pitfalls to look out for. Facing the same direction does not always mean the same amount of sun-value in a garden. For example, a sun-lover might be planted in full sun in the middle of plants which shade each others' roots. The same plant, facing the same direction but planted against a wall, will have to cope with drier and warmer conditions.

Even a small garden will have many microclimates, depending, for example, on whether they receive more or less sun or wind, or morning rather than afternoon shade. If a plant does not thrive, a first measure can

be to move it and see if it improves. One side of a large pot or a shrub will give more shelter than the other, for instance. Study your space well. Grey plants will enjoy the fullest sun whereas the large echeveria hybrids, gasterias and haworthias prefer partial sun, even shade. Not to be forgotten is the material that surrounds a plant. Paving will radiate more heat than grass.

This *Aloe suprafoliata* rejoices in the name 'Brylcream Bill'; the leaves can be kept flat by watering sparingly.

Placing a plant to best advantage

Some succulents have architectural features which need careful placement to be displayed to best advantage. The leaves of *Aloe polyphylla* from Lesotho in southern Africa, for instance, grow in a whorl to 60 cm (24 in) wide, and are arranged in a remarkable spiral (worth growing if you can get hold of it). Make sure that you can look down into it, say, beside a path—seen side-on some of the impact of the spiralling leaves is lost. *Aloe suprafoliata* has

The dramatic whirling growth of *Aloe polyphylla*.

An unknown echeveria species which looks very different when grown 'hard' and 'soft'.

About 2 m (7 ft) long, this stapeliad loops through a shadehouse looking like an alien visitor.

narrow leaves that grow sideways, one on top of each other. They are parted sharply down the middle. I call mine 'Brylcream Bill'. The dapper Fred Astaire of the succulent world, it needs to be seen side-on for best advantage. A beautiful feature of some strong-spined agaves is the imprint left by a leaf on the underside of a new leaf, called 'diapering'. On a plant placed at eye-level it is a beautiful feature.

Some echeverias are seen to advantage if you can look down into their heart, but graptopetalums develop graceful sinuous stems which are often best seen from the side. The egg-like leaves of pachyphyllums are interesting from whichever angle you view them, but if you are able to place them high you will be able to look up into their very beautiful but heavily nodding flowers. *Echeveria runyonii* 'Topsy Turvy' has incurved grey leaves, and when it sends up a sturdy, pretty wand of soft pink flowers it looks magnificent, but if you are able to place it where the afternoon sun passes behind it, it lights up in a spectacular fashion.

Closing a garden down for an absence

Plants in containers should be soaked and placed in semi-shade or shade where it is cooler and where they will dry out more slowly. If an automatic sprinkler system is in use, take care to place succulents on the periphery of the spray, as too much water on the leaves can cause them to rot. Cut off any flower spikes that

Echeveria 'Worfield Wonder'.

will flower in your absence, as flower spikes use water, and the plant might as well put all its energy into beautiful leaves that you can enjoy on your return.

Greenhouses and shadehouses

A greenhouse made from glass or polycarbonate is useful if you wish to grow succulents (and other plants) that might otherwise be marginal in your area. In a cold climate it can protect them from excessive cold and frost, and it can be heated. In a tropical climate a greenhouse may not need to have sides at all, its function being to prevent the plants receiving rain when it is not desirable and to allow air to circulate if humid. A greenhouse can provide shade in summer if the panes are made of light-diffusing material or covered with whitewash. It is essential in hot weather to have ventilation at both ends, as on a hot still day the temperature inside a greenhouse can soar disastrously. A poor friend of mine dashed back from work just two hours after leaving home. His greenhouse doors were closed and the temperature had risen to 50°C (122°F). He lost every one of his treasured cacti and succulents.

A greenhouse defines a private 'territory' for the owner. It can be locked if there are small children around or there is a possibility of rare plants being stolen. Plant collectors who wish to achieve a 'specimen' cactus, lithops or euphorbia, or a plant that has a fine 'talc' on its leaves, find a greenhouse is essential to protect them from rain, sun and cold. Glass keeps out birds, protecting plants from being pecked

or landed on. On the other hand, when insect-scavenging birds are excluded, insects that thrive on still air, such as mealy bugs and red spider mite, can become a problem. Some succulents can be very fussy, and if one is not thriving, moving it to another position in the greenhouse, perhaps higher where it is hotter, or into heavier shade, can sometimes work wonders. If you have a greenhouse it is essential once a year to take every plant out and have a thorough clean-out, brushing out loose soil and fallen leaves.

Often more useful in Mediterranean climates are shadehouses and sheds. Solidly built uprights covered over with shadecloth are often enough to diffuse sunlight while allowing air to circulate. Slats also provide the soft dappled shade that many succulents prefer. The great Victorian ferneries did this superbly. I know many home-built sheds which are full of character. If there are walls they are usually of wood, which mostly appears to have been scrounged, likewise the windows, and they gape and warp, allowing plenty of air to circulate. There can be the odd bit of corrugated iron (usually on the shady side, where the sun doesn't heat it too much). There are rails at an easy height from which to suspend plants, and benches placed at the correct height for the owner to easily tend the plants. Owners and plants exude happiness. To be invited into such a sanctuary is an honour that should not be taken lightly. It is a compliment given only to those who are likely to understand something of what they will see, and any information gleaned is always as valuable as a gold nugget.

Greenhouses are not for everyone. I like to live in harmony with my climate, and if I cannot make a plant thrive in the open, I will not grow it. Remarkably few plants defeat me, but if I encounter an unusual or rare plant (that is, possibly hard to grow) I ask the seller for hints, and carefully evaluate the microclimates at my disposal. I do not have any lithops, for instance, because I cannot keep them dry when dormant. In winter I keep inside a tray … well, two … of newly ordered plants, or cuttings that need particular care. I need the discipline of not having a greenhouse, as I know if I had one it would be full in five minutes.

Hazards
Sun and sunburn
The idea of a succulent being sunburnt can seem laughable. Succulents are adapted to survive in more

sun than most plants, but occasionally, in the first sudden burst of extremely fierce sun at the beginning of summer, even they can become sunburnt—the water 'boils' inside the leaf, leaving a scar. In studies of grapevines it was found that the first really strong sun stimulated their leaves to produce proteins which gave them protection; it may be that something similar occurs with succulents. Like us, they can lose the ability to tolerate sun after a long winter, if they have been grown inside or even been moved temporarily inside, or if they have been in the shade for too long. So never move a plant straight from shade to full sun. If you have bought a plant from a shaded nursery, find a halfway house for a few days. This also applies to cuttings that have come from a sheltered place, or have been kept inside for a while. If sunburn occurs, feed and water the plant, leave the burnt leaves on so they continue to feed it, and wait for new, clean leaves to grow. Sunburn occurs less often on succulents grown in the ground.

Rain, hail and frost

Succulents are found in dry scrubland, deserts and mountains, and most can withstand the vagaries of a Mediterranean climate, including light frost. Remember that deserts often have temperatures below −5°C (22°F) at night. Succulents hate to be waterlogged *at the same time* as being hit by frost, so it is wise to keep plants fairly dry if there is a chance of frost, but giving just enough water to keep their adventitious roots alive through winter. Adventitious roots remain dormant, ready to take advantage of the smallest shower, and if such a plant is kept too dry the little roots die and are unable to drink in the first rain.

Long periods of sunless winter can sometimes cause problems in succulents with densely packed leaves or those whose hairs are designed to capture the slightest mist or dew, but are unnerved by a torrent. Most gardens have drier parts, often near the walls of the house, to which pots can be moved for a while. Specialist growers stand some plants on a heat mat in winter, which can be kept at about 10–14°C (50–58°F), and will also warm the surrounding air.

Hail can sometimes 'pock' a plant. Dry the holes as much as you can (with a tissue, if necessary, on a treasured plant) to encourage the growth of protective scar tissue and the plant will quickly grow new leaves. Water sitting in the holes can cause the plant to rot, so

Echeveria 'Mauna Loa' with sunburn on the lower leaves.

if possible move the plant to a drier place, especially if it is still raining. Keep fed and watered (from below), and it will soon be on the road to recovery.

If succulents are kept in a place where the temperature does not vary for long periods of time, such as in a hospital, they can become sick. Remember that succulents breathe at night and that this process is triggered by a drop in temperature. If the temperature remains constant, the plant can actually suffocate; if possible put it outside occasionally for a cool spell.

Pests

In spite of the frightening list below, succulents are relatively pest free, especially if they are part of a varied planting. Difficulties with succulents, as with any plants, are usually due to bad cultivation: a sick plant is always more vulnerable to disease than a strong one. However, if you grow a lot of any one plant together you are liable to get pests specific to that plant. In my case, mealy bug and weevils were not a problem until I began growing a large number of the same type of plant close together.

Insecticides

Never use oil-based sprays on succulent plants—they block the pores and kill the plants. Use a contact insecticide such as Clensel or tomato or rose dust, which can be scattered beneath pots to kill insects which often shelter under them. A longer term solution is to work a systemic insecticide into the top 2–3 cm (about 1 in) of the soil. When watered it will be taken up into the plant's system and kill any insect that feeds on it. Some plants grow quite happily even if affected, but other plants will look sickly. So, it is not the end of the world if your plant has bugs. A different approach is to use a product such as Seasol, which acts by strengthening the cell walls and thus not only reduces water lost through transpiration, but also has an anti-insect effect as the plants are harder for insects to chew.

Leaf mealy bug

Mealy bugs are the only insects which pose any serious problem for succulents. Mealy bug looks like small, fluffy white bundles of cotton wool, often nestled into the leaf axils deep within a plant. It can be scarcely noticeable at first glance. If you squash a bundle you will find a small, juicy black bug in the middle. It is hard to eradicate mainly because by the time you notice it, it is likely to have spread. A light infestation of the leaf mealy bug can spread to the roots. This is a particular nuisance in greenhouses with still air and few predators, but it can also attack plants crowded close together in an airless part of the garden, especially in dry years, or in dry shade. Swish the plant around in a pail of pyrethrum dip or Clensel.

Root mealy bug

This is more of a problem for succulents than leaf mealy bug because it is more difficult to eradicate. Root mealy bug looks like fluffy white patches on the roots, similar to mould. An infected plant will not die, but it will not thrive. It is more of a problem in pots than in plants grown in the ground. If possible, take cuttings and discard the roots and soil. Otherwise, tip the infected plant out of its pot or dig it up, lightly tease away infected soil (onto newspaper so you can throw it away and not spread infection) and soak the roots, better still the whole plant, in a solution of Rogor (dimethoate) for at least a day, then replant. Rogor is dangerous and should be kept *only* for root mealy bug. Do not breathe in the fumes as they are carcinogenic. If you come across an infected plant it is worth checking nearby plants in case the pest has spread, as ants will carry it, even from pot to pot.

If you re-use pots that have had infected plants in them, scrub and rinse them and disinfect with potassium permanganate (Condy's crystals). Dissolve the crystals in a basin of water, pile in the pots and let soak—but wear rubber gloves to prevent your hands turning brown. You can use bleach if you prefer, and even a trip through the dishwasher will disinfect them effectively.

Prevention is much better than cure as root mealy bug can be hard to get rid of. If you acquire a plant from an unfamiliar source—such as a fete—ease it out of the pot and inspect it carefully. It can be sensible to quarantine it for a while or, best of all, take cuttings and throw away the parent plant and the soil it is growing in. Be careful even if you know the source.

Hopping spider

This little creature, brownish and about 5 mm (1/4 in) long, is sometimes seen on plants affected by mealy bug. It is not a pest, indeed, it is to be encouraged as it feeds on the bug and helps keep the plant clean.

Aphids

Spray with Seasol. It acts on the surface cells of the leaves, making them stronger and harder for insects to chew, and has a long-lasting repellent effect. Aphids are carried to nectar by ants, so if you have aphids, inspect for ants and deal with them also.

Snails and ants

A square of perforated zinc or flywire placed over the hole of a pot before filling it with soil can prevent insects getting in and setting up colonies. Pyrethrum powder scattered underneath a pot (so that it cannot be seen) or around a plant can work wonders with ants and crawlies.

Ants are great spreaders of disease and pests, so do not take their presence lightly. They sometimes carry earth onto the crown of a succulent. If they do this in wet weather the plant can rot and die, but symptoms are soon obvious and can be quickly dealt with.

Succulents are occasionally attacked by snails.

Once the snails manage to rasp a hole in a leaf, they seem to come back for more and produce unsightly damage. Snail bait scattered around the base of a plant or a dog-bowl of beer, sunk to its rim nearby in the flowerbed, should clear them up.

Soldier beetles, weevils, earwigs, cockchafers

If leaves have shallow nibbles down the edges it can be caused by a small weevil that comes out at night. If you suspect weevils, go out with a torch at night to pick them off and destroy them, but they are shy and hard to catch. Their larvae can eat roots and if when repotting you find a plant has smaller roots than you remember, check for larvae: they look like curved jelly beans and wriggle if you touch them. If they are present, scatter a systemic insecticide on the top 2–3 cm (1 in) of the soil. Water will carry this down to the plant's roots, it will be taken up into the plant and kill any insect that chews on it. Carbaryl is also highly effective.

Simple remedies often work well. For example, a piece of newspaper screwed up and left beside a pot overnight will gather earwigs which can then be thrown away, and crawling beetles cannot get into a pot if it is raised on little pot feet (even cork segments glued under a pot lift it high enough that beetles cannot get in).

Sciaria fly, wasps and birds

Sciaria flies are like tiny vinegar flies (fruit flies): they hover around your plants as if they were bad fruit, lay eggs in them—and then the hatching larvae can eat the plant from the inside. Along with many insects, they hate the smell of margarine, so I clear them by putting a spoonful of margarine on a saucer in the middle of my plants. Unglamorous, unorthodox, but highly effective. A prettier way to control them in an enclosed space is to use a carnivorous plant, such as *Pinguicula morganensis* x *ehlersae*, whose sticky leaves attract, capture and *dissolve* the flies. The pinguicula is very pretty; little mauve flowers similar to an African violet bounce almost all year above pale green succulent leaves that look like coiled turbans.

Birds love pecking plants such as lithops with their clear glassy tops but can often be deterred by installing a big plastic snake on the ground nearby.

For wasps, pitcher plants (*Nepenthes* species) are highly effective, but they will probably need to be placed inside or under shelter during the winter months if you have cold winters; they thrive in the protection of a conservatory.

Watering

The simplest way to reduce water consumption in a garden is to avoid plants that need a lot of watering. Failing that, group high-water plants in one part of a garden where they can receive special treatment. Grouping together plants which have similar needs, for example, low water, high water (this could be tomatoes and lettuces), high humus, summer water, is common sense. Thoughtful gardeners do this naturally, as plants *look* so much better when their particular needs are met—and besides, it makes for easier gardening than having to remember to give different care to one particular plant amongst a group.

Many people plant Australian native trees, expecting them to use less water than a deciduous tree. But a young eucalypt soaks up vast amounts of water. It has evolved to suck up every last drop of water whenever it is available, leaving the surrounding soil drier than the equivalent deciduous tree would do. This ability is put to use controlling water seepage in such places as King's Canyon National Park in Central Australia. Water and sewage from the tourist centre is pumped into shallow evaporation pans which are surrounded by rows of eucalypts which suck it up, thus preventing tourist waste water upsetting the surrounding water levels.

A deciduous tree is often a more water-efficient choice for a town garden in a Mediterranean climate, as it needs water mainly in the spring when most rain falls. Its water use tapers off over summer and autumn, it needs no water when dormant, and it mulches its own roots with its leaf-fall. It will use less water than a eucalypt in the same spot.

Maximise the water-retentiveness of your soil by adding humus (compost or a bale of pea straw) and a good mulch. Check the soil levels; water will sink in better on flat surfaces than on a slope. You might find it helpful to terrace a slope.

Water crystals can be added to the soil surrounding a high-water plant to make a damp spot, and soil wetters can be applied with a hose when watering (take care to hose off any that gets onto the leaves). Soil wetters are said to be effective for six months; they may help but in my experience they do not work miracles.

Watering plants in the garden

Succulents are low-water plants, not no-water plants. Succulents can survive for a time without water, indeed many of them like to become nearly dry between waterings, but no plant can survive without water.

Avoid wetting the leaves, as this can cause rot. It is best to water in the morning, so the sun has a chance to evaporate water accidentally sprayed onto leaves. Be careful of watering in the middle of the day because a droplet of water sitting on a leaf can magnify the sun's rays and burn a hole. Watering in the evening can be a very serene occupation, indeed some people swear—with gin and tonic in hand—that it is *most* pleasurable. But avoid wetting the leaves of densely leaved plants in particular because the sun will not be able to evaporate the excess water.

How often should you water? And what happens if they get too little water? The plants will tell you by looking perky when they are happy. In summer you know it is hot and you are on your guard for dry plants. The most dangerous time for succulents is winter, when you are not 'thinking water'. Be careful to check occasionally, especially young plants or plants in small pots, even if it has rained.

Watering pots

Rule of thumb is check once a week in summer, once a fortnight in winter. You may not always need to water. Soil should always be at least 1 cm (3/8 in) below the pot rim for easy watering. A pot standing in shade will need less water than the same pot in full sun; however, take into account that the fierce midday sun will strike mainly on the rim of a pot, heating it less that if it receives the full strength of the low afternoon sun on the broad expanse of its side. In winter, if there is a long period of rain, pots can be moved under an eave (there is usually one side of the house that is away from the prevailing rain). Sometimes water can run through soil that has been in a pot a long time, scarcely wetting it, so that very little water actually gets to the roots. If you suspect this is happening, immerse the pot in a bowl or a wheelbarrow full of water, and see how long it bubbles. If it is still bubbling slowly after five minutes there is a problem. To combat this, you can repot or topdress with a spoonful of a wetting product. Next time you pot add coir and compost to the mix to help water absorption. Especially in summer, the occasional good soak acts like a tonic on all plants in pots.

Sometimes soil will splash up onto leaves when you are watering, which can look ugly. There are two ways of dealing with this. Reduce the volume of water and use a spray gun on your hose, or put decorative stones round the plant to deflect the water. Dedicated plant collectors sometimes lay a 3 cm (1˝ in) square of zinc mesh on the soil beside the plant. The water trickles through but the mesh breaks the force of the water jet and prevents soil splashing up onto the leaves.

Mounding

Italian gardeners, in particular, use a water conservation technique called mounding that has been effective since the days of the Romans. It was used by the Aztecs to grow maize and is still used widely in the Far East in rice paddies. Mounding involves piling soil neatly to form a moat so that the water meant for a particular place will soak into the area for which it is intended.

This technique is also useful on slopes, where the earth can be terraced or the soil banked up in a half-moon on the downhill side of a plant to ensure the water does not run off before it has soaked in. Neatly done, this looks decorative, and uses water economically. It also makes it easier to cater for the needs of an individual plant, for instance, a citrus plant growing in the middle of herbs might need more water than its companions, or a tomato plant might deserve more pampering than the decorative succulents that surround it.

Mulching

The essential principle behind mulching is that it protects the surface from drying out quickly so that water is more available in the soil for the roots to absorb. Mulch can also function as a weed-suppressor, and in the case of an organic mulch can be a source of nutrients and humus as it breaks down. The options are many. Shredded bark is often used although, while it can look good in a rural setting as the initial deep brown fades to a soft grey, and it is cheap, it is not nutritious and can also be a fire hazard. Softer materials such as pea straw, peanut husks and sugar cane mulch will slowly break down and enrich the soil. When applying mulch keep it away from the stem of a plant otherwise it can cause it to rot. People often tip grass clippings on the garden as a mulch, but they tend to form an impermeable mat which prevents water getting to the roots of the plants. It is best to compost grass clippings before using them as mulch. If do you use them fresh, make sure they do not rest up against trunks and stems, as the clippings can cause ringbarking as they break down.

Inorganic mulches such as stones, stone chips or

gravel can be decorative. Pebbles come in many different colours and can add to the impact of a garden: pale plants enhanced by black stones, or dark plants set off by white stones. By the sea, seashells can give a delightfully casual look.

Grooming

Succulents look best if they are regularly groomed. Some grow from the top and can develop a 'skirt' of dead leaves. Sometimes a plant will send roots out into the dead leaves, which forms a natural compost. This is especially noticeable in spreading plants, which can crawl over a rock, for instance, where there is no soil. In such cases leave the dead leaves well alone. A few aloes keep a skirt of old leaves, a mechanism to keep sun off the main trunk. If you are tempted to tidy too much, just 'talk' to your plant and see what it 'says' to you. As you walk around your pots checking them for water, it is a good idea to carry a plastic shopping bag, and remove any dead leaves or spent flower spikes, checking as you go for food needs and bugs.

Dead seed heads often look dramatic, but if they are unsightly or hard to remove while still green, cut off the main length and remove the rest when they have dried out a little. A large, long pair of medical tweezers is invaluable for picking out dry petals, thistle seeds and other bits which might have blown into the centre of a plant. Tweezers can also be used to remove weeds from deep within an interesting clump so that it is not unduly disturbed. Never plunge your fingers into a plant if there is a risk of making a mark on it. My succulents must look cuddly—I am always amazed at how many people want to feel the silky surface of a plant, leaving shiny, smudgy finger and thumb prints.

Labelling

Why label? Labels can store a lot of information: the name of the plant, when it was re-potted, fertilisers used, etc. If you are the sort of gardener who likes knowing the names of your plants it can be helpful to be able to check quickly. Sometimes a plant looks so different when grown in another way that you will not believe it could possibly be the same. *Echeveria* 'Zorro', for instance, was a sensational near-black one year grown in garden soil with a handful of cow manure. The next year, put into a container with other plants, potting mix and a chemical fertiliser, it looked almost green. If it had not had a label I would have been tempted to think I had made a mistake. A packet of sturdy plant labels, plastic, or better still, metal, is essential. For small pots, or to label a large number of spares, I cut a white plastic ice-cream container into wedges. The plastic is thin and will last only a few years, but makes a low-cost emergency label. Aluminium venetian blind slats are very good cut into lengths—use a sharp-tipped cheap biro to impress the name permanently into the metal.

'Permanent' markers can sometimes be impermanent, but the Sharpie brand of pen seems to be truly permanent, as is a waxy pencil. Labels need not be visible—they can be tucked down on the near side of a pot. Birds scratching for worms can uproot labels in the garden so it is a good idea to keep a key plan of a complicated planting in your garden notebook, as nothing is more annoying than losing the name of a plant.

Keeping a record

I have a large format cash ledger in which I record details of each new plant—where it came from, the cost, any information or growing hints which came with it. I add a tiny sketch, enough to help identify it if I should lose a label. I add cultivation notes as I come across them in books, the season of flowering and so on. If a plant dies or I discard it, I add a Death Notice, noting what I think went wrong so I do not make the same mistake again. The whole book gives me the greatest pleasure. After fifteen years it has become an anthology of dear friends and past passions, a record of triumphs and defeats.

Can I eat my succulents?

Do *not* eat succulents. Many succulents contain high levels of alkaloids, some of which are carcinogens.

Succulents close their stomata during the day and open them to breathe the cooler, less drying night air. They metabolise slowly during the day. Certain succulents have been tasted at different times during the day, and their taste is completely different hour by hour. I know of a kelpie sheepdog that eats his owners' succulents, but only at about 11 am, and it might be that at that particular time that particular plant has something the dog needs

The nutritional and curative qualities of *Aloe vera* have been well explored. At flowering time certain Mexican agaves store great amounts of starches, preparatory to sending up their vast flower spike, and at this stage can be fermented to make an alcoholic spirit. But there is a lot of local lore and experience involved in picking the precise moment to harvest, the preparation is complex and precise, and there are no records to tell us how many of the indigenous population died before they found ways to safely consume the result. Stick to tequila from the bottle shop.

Addiction

This is a serious problem with succulents, and not one on which I can give advice. Succulents are so very beautiful that you will always come across yet another that Cannot Be Left Behind. But, with a bit of luck, a sympathetic Other and a little bit of space, this addiction will be more of a pleasure than a problem. I partly solved the problem of space by sending away for a mail-order, green, powder-coated metal, four-tier bookcase kit. (The instructions began humorously, 'Easy assembly'.) The top layer gets full sun, good for cacti, the lower shelves are partially shaded by the plants above, and all can be seen at a glance. It makes the perfect nursery and infirmary. It stands out in all weathers and is still neat, unrusted and useful after six years.

Troubleshooting: Sad plants and how to make them happy

This is a quick summary. If a plant looks bad, or sad, have a very close look at it. Succulents are slow to show they are sick, and it could be that the plant is showing the effects of an event a few weeks previously, so think back—was there a sudden change in conditions?

1 It could need a feed If the leaves look yellow, give it some liquid fertiliser and leave for three weeks. Succulents need magnesium: a dose of Epsom salts (magnesium sulphate) can do wonders.

2 It might be too dry Likely if the leaves are crinkly and soft to the touch, or have died back at the tips. If you think that it should have had sufficient water, check that the water is actually getting to the roots—does the water 'ball' and roll off the soil? Submerge a pot in water and watch how much it bubbles. If it is still bubbling after five to ten minutes, the soil is the problem. A soak

will cure matters temporarily. Substandard potting mixes are often the culprit. In the ground, give the plant a good soak, wait a week and check again.

3 It might be old And just plain tired. Some plants perform best when young (geraniums are an example of this). Rejuvenate by taking cuttings.

4 Check the roots If the plant has been in a pot for a very long time, the roots might be congested. Tap it out. If the roots are densely matted and it has grown into a splendid old specimen, 'tickle' some of the old earth away, mix some new soil with a little fertiliser and repot in a larger pot. Succulents that offset, such as haworthias, can easily become congested. In this case, pull the plant apart, retain only the best bits and replant. If you have kept a pot sitting in a saucer of water, check the roots in case they have rotted. If you like the look of a saucer put it upside down so it does not hold water—succulents do not like to stand in a puddle.

A good way to store small, rare plants and spares.

5 Patchy leaves The problem could be insects or sunburn. Sunburn usually only happens on the first very hot day in spring or when a plant is first moved into the sun after it has been growing inside or in shade. It is rarely a problem with in-ground plants. Water droplets can also concentrate the sun and leave small burn marks which will grow out. Use pyrethrum spray if you suspect insects.

6 It looks sick Check for leaf and root mealy bug. This occurs most often in sheltered places and when plants are kept on the dry side. Fluffy white bundles in the leaf axils? Spray with insecticide (never oil-based on succulents). Examine the roots. Soft white spots like mildew? This is the dreaded root mealy bug (it is more common in pots than in the ground). Tickle away the soil, and soak in pyrethrum insecticide or Rogor (some say it is the only cure). The best way to get rid of root mealy bug is to take cuttings and put them in new soil, throw away all infected soil, and sterilise the pot. It is a good idea to check neighbouring plants.

7 Black and dirty flower spikes or leaves Probably aphis. If there are small black insects, spray with pyrethrum and put pyrethrum powder underneath the pot or in surrounding soil. Ants are usually the culprit—they 'farm' aphis—so treat the ants as much as the aphis.

8 Leaves are nibbled If it is snails there will be a trail of slime. Delicate shallow nibbles on the edges of leaves can be beetles which feast at night. Go out with a torch at night and remove, or sprinkle a systemic insecticide, mix it into the top of the soil and water in. Treat the surrounds, dust pyrethrum under a pot or around the plant. There is always an unexpected local hazard, such as deer, rabbits, parrots, possums, which often choose one plant only, but then make a feast of it.

9 It looks lanky, leans and won't flower It might not be getting enough light. Lack of sun can prevent a plant from flowering or cause the whole plant to lean towards the sun. Prune back overhanging trees or shrubs or move the plant to a sunnier position.

10 It died If it was a new plant your conditions might have been unsuitable. If it was an old plant, was there a change in conditions? Did you water it? Suspect drainage and check. Maybe it is deciduous, and will sprout in spring? Perhaps someone forgot to tell you they had given it a handful of fertiliser, and not knowing this you have repotted it with too much? Someone washed the car and threw the detergent water over the garden? The most unlikely explanations can sometimes be right.

2 Propagating and Acquiring Succulents

Succulent plants mostly duplicate themselves fast and grow quickly when conditions are suitable. It is easy and rewarding to propagate them. Duplicates are useful as presents, swaps or as a hedge against disaster. It can be interesting to grow cuttings of the same succulent in different ways—in a pot or in the ground, in sun or in shade, 'hard' in poor soil, fertilised rarely, watered irregularly, or 'soft' in good soil, fertilised carefully, watered regularly, because they can look strikingly different.

Cuttings

Always allow a succulent cutting to dry for at least a day. A protective callus will grow over the wound and prevent it rotting.

You can be confident that a plant grown from a cutting will have the exact DNA of the parent. A plant grown from seed might have been fertilised by pollen from another plant, and so is more likely to vary from the parent. Growing plants put into a different soil may not thrive, whereas seed will germinate and happily grow in many different kinds of soil. When sowing very fine seed, mix with a spoonful of sand. It is then easy to see that you are sowing it evenly.

A cutting should be cut cleanly—a ragged cut will harbour water and be more likely to rot. If someone snaps off a cutting for you, recut the rough break when you get home. Secateurs or a hobby knife will do a good job. Remember, always allow cuttings to dry in a cool place for a day or two before planting them.

An exception

Euphorbia caput-medusae has radiating, fleshy arms which look like a bunch of octopus tentacles; they form a flat star about 40–60 cm (16–24 in) wide. A mature specimen will either make your eyes pop out of your head with amazed joy or squeeze them shut in horror. If you take a cutting from this plant (and one or two other euphorbias of similar extraordinary form), you will get a strange bunch of sideways 'fingers' that will not come true to the shape of the parent. In this case, wait for seed.

Leaf cuttings

Plants with juicy leaves will often grow from a detached leaf. The leaf will use its stored water to survive until it puts out roots. Crassulas, graptoverias and sedums are particularly easily propagated this way. Usually species echeverias will grow from a leaf, though some hybridised ones may not. There is an exception to every rule, and the best thing is to try and see what happens. Choose a leaf in full growth, not an old one that is just about to be shed and not a small, immature one.

A leaf of an oak-leaved kalanchoe will develop plantlets after four weeks.

Kalanchoes

Carefully break off a leaf, place it on the soil in a pot in a sheltered place, and be patient. After about two weeks you will notice fine roots sprouting, or sometimes plantlets beginning to grow from it. Some kalanchoes have little adventitious plants along the sides of their leaves—children love to see how the roots of these wave in the air. Do not grow this kind if there is a chance of their escaping into the wild because they can spread disastrously.

Rosette succulents

There are two reasons you might need to take cuttings of these plants, which include *Graptoveria*, *Pachyphyllum* and *Pachyveria*. First, to renew the plant when it gets 'leggy', and second, to increase your supply of them. To rejuvenate a leggy plant, cut off its head, allow to dry and replant. To increase the number of plants, remove good strong leaves cleanly with a sideways pull from the parent plant, put somewhere cool and safe. After two weeks you will see tiny roots and a tiny plant growing from the end of the leaf that was attached to the parent. Cover the roots lightly with soil, and the new plant will flourish.

Root cuttings

Sometimes the best way to obtain a cutting from a plant with woody roots, such as the deciduous sedums, is to cut off a piece of the root. Cut a piece cleanly, and allow to dry, then plant in a sandy propagating mix.

Euphorbias

These can be propagated from seed, or from root or stem cuttings, depending on variety. They have a thick, latex-like sap which oozes for a few minutes before setting into a glassy cap which makes rooting slow. When you are ready to root a euphorbia cutting, make a fresh clean cut, and hold it under a tap for a few minutes until the sap has stopped oozing. The cut will heal, but the sap will not have formed a cap. Plant it in a pot, and it should grow roots. You can dip the cut end in sulphur powder or a rooting hormone if you wish, but euphorbias are slow rooters at the best of times, so be patient. Be careful not to get sap on your skin because some kinds are highly allergenic and can cause agony if the sap gets in your eye.

Beheading

This technique applies to echeverias in particular, which grow from the top. As they grow the lower leaves gradually die off, which can result in a rosette on top of a long stalk. Some, such as the carunculated *Echeveria* 'Paul Bunyan', have interesting markings on their stalks, which can grow to 50 cm (20 in) or so. The stalks are most decorative at this stage, but eventually the plant becomes top-heavy. Water the plant well a couple of days before, because the cut head will live off stored water until the roots grow. It will still grow if it is dry, but less enthusiastically. Use secateurs to cut off the head, leaving a 4 cm (1° in) stump. Leave the head aside for a week or so (balanced on an empty pot is ideal) so that it develops a callus and the roots can sprout unhindered. (At this stage the plant can be left out of the ground for a couple of weeks and can be easily put in the mail.) Once the callus has formed simply put the plant onto new soil and it will root within a few days.

If you want more echeverias, keep the remaining stalk watered, and on most varieties little plantlets will grow in a spiral all the way up the stem. Wait until these are at least as large as a walnut, then detach them gently, place them on soil or potting mix and they will root. If you remove them too early the

Pretty, pink *Echeveria* 'Perle von Nurnburg' has been cut off for re-rooting, leaving offsets that will grow on to form a clump.

Offsets are small plants produced from the parent by a stalk or an underground runner. Left alone this can result in a highly desirable and decorative cluster or can end up looking untidy. Look hard at your plant and decide whether it pleases you, or whether action is needed. Most offsets are easy to detach from the parent plant, and will root easily, but others remain attached to the parent for a long time. Agaves can sometimes develop numerous 'pups' around their base, which can detract from the impact of a specimen plant, in which case gently pull to detach them.

Swapping

I find swapping the most enjoyable way to get new plants. Gardeners' etiquette insists that if you are offered something you must offer something in return. You will be told why the plant you are offered is treasured, and given hints on growing it well.

Acquiring, with or without permission

Succulents are often found in neglected gardens simply because they are the only things that haven't died. Ask permission if possible. I have knocked on doors to ask for a plant, and have always gladly been given what I asked for, with a cheery conversation usually thrown in. Be fair—take a piece only if it does not spoil the plant, perhaps from the back, or from low down. Legally, you can take a piece of a plant if it spills through a fence onto a pathway which is public land, but if you take something from within a property, it is stealing. You are usually only tempted by something that looks good, which probably means it is growing well. Take note of the conditions that have suited it.

Mail order

Many gardening magazines have mail order nurseries listed in the back. Succulent suppliers are usually individual characters; some of their catalogues will be just a list of the varieties on offer, others will be twenty close-typed pages with descriptions. You may feel you do not know where to begin when you first look at all the unfamiliar names. If the choice is difficult, telephone the nursery for advice. Good nurseries know their stock, and if you describe the conditions under which you grow your plants and any preferences, they are often happy to send you a selection of their top

plantlets will not have enough stored water to tide them over until they have rooted, and can wither and die. Slice off carefully, leaving a bit of the inner green pith of the stalk adhering to the tough outer stem (to which the plantlet is attached). Dry off for a day, ideally dip in hormone rooting powder to ensure success. It is better to put these in a small pot to keep a close eye on them until they are rooted—a scratching bird in a flowerbed could spell disaster. Let them grow a little before potting on or planting out.

Division and offsets

Some succulents form clumps which eventually require thinning. Gasterias, for instance, sometimes look better if they can assert their strong shapes individually, rather than huddling in a cluster. Sometimes the stems can be fused together at ground level. Using a Stanley knife, cut firmly in a natural join between the plants and allow the divisions to form a callus before replanting.

suggestions, the Plants Most Likely to Succeed. About twenty years ago I sent off for '20 unnamed garden treasures'; they were cheap, and a triumph of extraordinary and beautiful 'bits' providing enjoyment to this day.

Plants sent by mail sometimes arrive in beautifully neat, wrapped packages, each with a label, as if the grower has farewelled each plant individually. Others come scrunched in newspaper with their names scrawled on the edge. I find it magical to open a tiny parcel which may well hold a plant that could become a friend and part of the fabric of my life. Keep a note of the names in case you get addicted and want to avoid duplications in future orders.

Some of the larger nurseries grow many, perhaps thousands, of plants they do not list. They keep alive a vast genetic bank, and they are always glad to take enquiries from a really interested client. They are also in touch with dedicated private collectors who have extensive collections, and will often be able to find an unusual plant. Occasionally, such a nursery will have an Open Day; get there if you can. I defy anyone to remain unawed by the extraordinary variety of plants treasured and preserved by such people.

There are some very good 'checklist' type of books. *Succulents: The Illustrated Dictionary 1 & 2*, by M. Sajeva and M. Costanzo (Cassell, London, 1994) is useful. Try to visit a succulent nursery or a website where you can see a wide range.

Catalogues

The number of succulent catalogues that can be accessed through the Internet is increasing so quickly that any list will be almost immediately out of date, but for Australia try:

• Rudi Schultz: tarrex@ozemail.com.au
• Paul Forster, PO Box 2171, Ashgrove West, Queensland 4060   email: paulforster@uq.net.au
• Bev Spiller: www.echeveriasinoz.com
• Collector's Corner: www.collectorscorner.com.au
• Geoff Mansell: www.exoticaplants.com.au—a good supplier of carnivorous plants
• Andoran Stud, Darkes Forest NSW 2508. They also sell a CD Rom showing 300 echeverias, graptoverias for $22.

Importing

Some countries, including Australia, have rigid plant quarantine laws. Your local post office has the relevant information. Plants from Australia can sometimes be sent overseas, but if an Australian wants to bring a plant into the country it has to go through a quarantine process. The Australian Quarantine Inspection Service (AQIS) is fairly expensive, and they usually keep the plants for three months. If you want a rare plant it is worth first making enquiries from dedicated local nurseries, as the plant you want is very likely to be in the country already. Many nurseries grow plants in small quantities which they do not list, or know of the existence of a particular plant in another nursery.

A few years ago I imported some plants and I found the quarantine process fascinating. I could visit my plants—disinfectant shoe bath before entering the quarantine house—whenever I wanted. Many of the plants being screened were imported for agricultural purposes, such as potatoes or vines. While I was there, one was found with a blight that could have wiped out a whole industry. AQIS grew my plants so hard I nearly cried, but they explained this was necessary to enable them to withstand the fierce regime of insecticidal spraying to which they were obliged to subject them. No harm was done, and they exploded into growth when I got them home and repotted them.

No one who has seen the dedication of the AQIS team would ever dream of smuggling in a plant. Many pests and diseases, such as the elm beetle and the horrid 'trigger weed', must have been introduced by plants smuggled into Australia. If you want to import a plant, obtain permission in advance as plants are confiscated if they arrive unexpectedly at customs.

• AQIS Emergency line from abroad: Tara Lee 613 8318 6987 at Nursery Stock, Melbourne Airport. Website: www.aqis.gov.au

• AQIS Melbourne: phone (03) 9310 3155; fax (03) 9920 1718
• AQIS Sydney: phone (02) 8805 1071
• AQIS Perth: (08) 9368 3460

3 Most Popular and Easily Grown

My top ten
Aeonium
Cacti
Cotyledon
Crassula
Echeveria
Euphorbia
Graptopetalum/Graptoveria
Haworthia
Kalanchoe
Sedum
Companion bulb: *Agapanthus*

This chapter lists some of the most popular, easily grown and easily obtainable succulent genera, each of which has large numbers of beautiful species, hybrids and cultivars, both for gardens and for pots. Cacti, though succulent, are not strictly succulent plants, but they are an important part of low-water gardening, so they take a bow.

Aeonium

Mainly from the Canary Islands and North Africa. Rosettes 5–25 cm (2–10 in) across, 30 cm–1 m (12 in–3 ft) high. They are winter growing, evergreen plants which can be grown equally well in sun or shade. They are pest free, so always seem to look fresh and well grown. Aeoniums have a particularly wide range

Many aeoniums, such as *A. urbicum* pictured here on the left, with *Agave attenuata*, purse up when dry in summer, but they still look interesting.

of leaf colour—green, black, mahogany, even variegated and hairy. The dark ones should be grown in sun for maximum colour. Most have yellow flowers. The stalk carrying the flowers will die after flowering, but small plants sprouting from the base will grow on for the next year. In summer, some green aeoniums rest, 'pursing up' until they are deeply cupped.

The large *A. urbicum* (sometimes incorrectly called *A. canariense*), stands 1 m (3 ft) high, and looks spectacular at the back of a border. I suspect that nearly all the various forms available in Australia are mostly hybrids. However, it is a truly splendid plant. Its rosettes have such a strong shape that it is amongst the most architectural of succulents and makes a superb focal point at the end of a vista, for instance. It enjoys full sun but in my garden also thrives in dry shade. At the end of summer I often cut off four or five stalks and plant them in a large pot. They quickly root to make an unusual pot plant.

I acquired my *A. urbicum* years ago when we stopped to buy a sack of potatoes from a farmer. As we lugged the potatoes back to the car I saw the most striking and beautiful plant with rosettes as large as dinner plates held high on strong stalks. It must have been preserved from times gone by (it appears in many of the gardens planted by the great colonial gardener Guilfoyle himself, say some), because this happened long before it appeared in any plant list that I had seen. I *had* to have it. I asked, I begged. I could have a piece, but only if I bought a *second* bag of potatoes. It takes a long time to eat two bags of potatoes, and eventually we had to heave a sack full of wobbly mauve tendrils onto the compost. It was worth it!

A friend who owns a gallery was sent a bunch of flowers for an opening. They died, but amongst them were three 75 cm (30 in) stalks of a spectacular *A. urbicum* which he kept in water for a further two months. When I saw them they looked utterly contemporary and quite glorious standing in a huge clear glass vase. Although they still looked as fresh as the day they were picked, in my friend's opinion they had become 'yucky' (roots were growing at the bottom), and he was glad to give them to me. I planted them in a pot at once. About six months later the rosettes produced enormous panicles of flowers about 60 cm (24 in) long. When they were half out I cut them and to my amazement had them inside for no less than six weeks, the flowers opening in succession so that they always looked crowd-stoppingly spectacular. Those three stalks had given ten months of enjoyment.

There are many interesting smaller aeoniums. Flat little *A. tabuliforme* (see Chapter 11, Shady Characters) grows best in shade or semi-shade. *A.* 'Abbey Brook' clumps into a neat bush; it is slightly variegated grey-silver and slightly hairy, which makes it shine in the sun. *A.* 'Suncup' is particularly pretty, and makes a small, puffy bush in two to three years. Its rosettes are variegated, and on some the variegation is so strong that that they are almost pure yellow so that the bush looks as if it is in flower even when it isn't. This is one to leave in a pot for years so it can mound up, and I find it does as well in full sun as in shade. The leaves of *A.* 'Tricolour' are green-yellow variegated with sharp red rims which make them appear electric; it is fairly slow to mound up but very beautiful. The flowers of these small aeoniums are a froth of whitish or yellowish stars; when the flowering stalk dies back, give it a quick trim and it will look as beautiful as ever. *A. lindleyi* has sticky fat leaves—an interesting small plant. *A. decora* could be described as 'sweet'; it has smoky grey-white leaves with the softest pink edges. I am not alone in finding it difficult to grow, so it is particularly galling on occasion to come across it growing in thickets in someone else's garden. It needs a good root run, grit and drainage. If you have the chance, try it. And good luck.

A. 'Sunburst' is a spectacular variegated aeonium 25 cm (10 in) across. Its green leaves have a strong white edge, making it look as it if has been painted. The stem can grow tall, so it has a 'lollipop' appearance when it gets to about 40 cm (16 in). It makes a stunning specimen in the ground or in a pot.

The darkest aeonium is the near-black *A. arboreum* 'Zwartkop', sometimes known as 'Schwarzkopf', which reaches 1 m (3 ft). It is blackest in full sun. I have grown it in the same small pot for eight years. Every spring I gently turn it out, and replace some of the soil with a mix of compost and cow manure. I do not topdress this particular plant, because a beautiful crust of moss has covered the soil—which makes it look positively *designer*! Each year I shorten half the stems, which then sprout new rosettes halfway down, producing a decorative double-layered look. The rosettes are tight and small and very black. When it is grown in the ground the rosettes expand dramatically,

Aeonium 'Zwartkop' and *A. urbicum* look fresh and pretty grown together; they are dwarfed by being crammed into one pot.

almost to the point of looking shaggy. A particularly beautiful effect can be obtained by planting cuttings of a green aeonium, such as *A. urbicum*, alternately with 'Zwartkop'. Do this in a container in late autumn and you will have a beautiful fresh-looking centrepiece all winter. *A. arboreum* var. *atropurpureum*, its green leaves mahogany-tipped, is not as dark as 'Zwartkop' but is a superb garden plant; its colour is a particularly good foil for green leaves. Both these make bushes to 1 m (3 ft), but can become top heavy, so prune judiciously to prevent them toppling over.

Some aeoniums are stemless, their large saucers hugging the ground, and an amazing effect could be achieved by planting short types in front of the tall ones.

Aeoniums are easily propagated in autumn and winter by cutting off a head with a few centimetres (2 in or so) of stalk. Small rosettes may sprout at the top of the remaining stalk if you keep it watered. Aeoniums can be hard to strike when they are in their summer dormant period.

For those who like the odd challenge watch out for the very pretty aeoniums previously known as greenovias, which look like a huddle of small green roses. They are good for rockeries. Their leaves, like those of some aeoniums, purse up or die down in summer.

Cacti

Central Americas. These vary in size from huge, fast-growing ones to small, slow-growing specimens useful in tiny gardens, and provide excellent contrast and texture in low-water gardens. Some cacti are almost as wide as they are tall, such as *Echinocactus grusonii*, the Golden Ball cactus (sometimes rudely referred to as Mother-in-law's Cushion), which can reach 1 m (3 ft) high and round. Many, such as the larger varieties of Prickly Pear (*Opuntia*) and *Cereus* are large, 4 m (14 ft) and architectural with strong upright corrugations. *Cereus peruvianus* 'monstrous form' is warty and compelling, with the presence of a small tree in a garden. The *Trichocereus* cacti, shorter at 1– 2 m (3–7 ft), flower magnificently when the conditions are to their liking. Cacti need well-drained soil and respond remarkably to food and kindness, but most

Trichocereus cacti give brilliant, long-lasting displays of flowers; they have hybridised freely in this hot garden.

can be kept small by judicious neglect if that is desired.

Cacti prefer dry air, and are prone to rot if the air is humid for long periods. If you live in a tropical climate and want a cactus effect, explore euphorbias. A case of parallel evolution—many euphorbias (which are mostly from Africa) could be mistaken for cacti. I have seen spectacular 2–3 m (7–10 ft) stands of *Euphorbia trigona*, looking for all the world like a Mexican candelabra cactus, thriving in tropical Darwin.

Some cacti are frost tolerant; lists of these appear at the end of Chapter 10, Shady Characters.

Cactus spines vary in colour: red, yellow, black and white. Those with white spines look spectacular if planted so the setting sun shines from behind and lights up the spines. Cacti are specialist country, and as I have not grown many I will not venture to give advice except to say that with their solid shapes they are the 'full stops' of a succulent garden and should be included whenever possible.

Cacti are often grown on windowsills. If they are neglected, starved of food and water and sufficient

A neglected cactus sometimes goes mad when suddenly given good care.

light, say in an office, they can grow weedy and elongated. They will never regain the characteristic rounded shape of a normal cactus even if put back into sun. If you have a stressed plant like this, do not throw it out. Give it regular soaks in dilute fertiliser and put it back into a good light, and if you are lucky it will sprout little cacti all over the surface and become a highly ornamental 'freak'. I saw a 1 m (3 ft) high

barrel cactus that had been given kind treatment after neglect—it had sprouted little orange-sized cacti all over its exterior, to hilarious effect.

Cotyledon

South Africa; to 50 cm (20 in), and widely grown. The grey ones grow as happily in light shade as in sun, the green ones need sun. They are hugely useful landscaping plants and they seem to thrive on neglect. *C. orbiculata* has beautiful round, silvery grey leaves like little paddles, and is almost the whitest plant in the garden. The leaves of *C.* 'Silver Waves', also grey, are wavy. It is often confused with *C. undulata,* which has a distinctly crimped edge. *C. macrantha,* which has just been reclassified as *C. orbiculata* var. *orbiculata,* has green leaves which grow upright with an attractive red rim around the edge, and a tall head of red flowers. Perhaps one should simply talk of *C. orbiculata* 'green form' and 'grey form' to help those unfamiliar with the name changes. The stems are soft and as they age they bend over gracefully and continue growing, forming a most attractive sprawling tumble.

I saw a stand of the grey *C. orbiculata* looking quite glorious and ablaze with flowers. The owner sniffed: 'They are such a mess, I think I'm going to pull them up.' I looked surprised and asked how long they had been there—thirty years. They had received no water or food in that time. I thought they deserved a medal. A memorable stand of the green form sat unwatered beside a farm gate in the middle of nowhere, flowering their hearts out. Their roots probably received some shelter from the surrounding low wild grasses, but it was survival in the face of adversity. Admirable. Cotyledons grow from the top and old leaves shrivel and drop away cleanly. An old stand can quickly be rejuvenated by cutting off the heads, pulling up old stalks, scattering a handful of fertiliser and replanting the heads.

Cotyledons are superb in pots and need only an occasional watering. They are the sort of plant that neglected look good, but when tended, occasionally renewed, and fed, look glorious. The courtyard of an elderly lady I know has a grey cotyledon in a beautiful, inherited Wedgwood-style pot, black with white applied figures. After the hottest run of days the plant stands cool and elegant, and I know it gets only intermittent care. I have a concrete tub of this cotyledon which forms a striking focal point at the

Cotyledon macrantha: hot, neglected, still lovely.

end of a path which turns around to the compost-and-dustbin-land at the back. I am embarrassed even to think when I last fed or renewed it. If I remember, it gets a splash of water after the tomatoes on a hot day. I mention this because, even as neglected as it is, the tub still looks good.

Cotyledons have beautiful flowers which grow from the centre of the head and are held high above the plant in midsummer. The pink, mealy flowers of *C. orbiculata* or the red bells of *C. orbiculata* var. *orbiculata* hang downwards like a chandelier, and on a hot Christmas table, surrounded with grey foliage, it is hard to imagine anything more Christmassy.

As in all succulent genera there are unusual types—hairy or variegated—worth looking out for. Some are very slow-growing but beautiful. *C. orbiculata* var. *oophylla* has a small, grey, lozenge-shaped leaf with a maroon line on the end as if an elf had been let loose with a crayon. It is slow to mound, but after three years it begins to build up to a neat and exquisite plant. For a person who has only a small garden such slow growth comes as a relief. Cotyledons are almost the perfect plant; they have few enemies and therefore always glow with health. They feature also in the Chapter 11, Shady Characters and Chapter 12, Succulents for Flowers.

Crassula

This genus spreads from South Africa to southern Arabia. Small to medium. If you think a 'crassula' is the bore you met at that party last week, think again. *Crassula* means 'thick', but this refers to their solid, enduring leaves. Crassulas range from desert dwellers to water plants. Bushes or carpeters, they have leaves of every possible colour and form. Most are tough and easy to grow, and they can be used as tumblers or as specimens. Their flowers are usually tiny but numerous and froth to very pretty effect. *C. coccinea*, introduced by the Dutch in 1701, is grown for its flowers. The bush, to 30 cm (12 in) high, is not particularly distinguished, but the flowers in early summer are a stunning pure red. It grows well by the sea and in poor soil.

A friend from the Philippines noticed I did not have a Money Tree (*C. ovata*) beside my front door and was as shocked as if I had run away with the vicar. Everyone *knows* that without a Money Tree a house will have bad luck. She gave me one called 'Hummel's Sunset' which grows like a small tree; its leaves are a variegated green and yellow with a touch of red on the edges. Pretty, and with soft pink flowers in winter, it will grow in shade, but colours best in strong light. I have seen a plain dark green, glossy variety with handsome, strong foliage surviving in an inhospitable stairwell where it looks bright and cheery with the occasional feed and water. (The very similar *Portulacaria afra* is also said to have good luck qualities.)

One of the most delightful crassulas is *C. arborescens*, a small shrub to 40 cm (16 in). Its flat, paddle-shaped leaves are a soft grey-green with a plum rim and decorative, prominent, plum dots—the pores—on the leaves. Slow-growing and tidy, it takes about two years to mound up to a most attractive specimen. In the garden it is a grand foil for a variegated aloe, or plants with fine, dissected leaves. It makes an undemanding pot plant, and would be good on a sheltered (not windy) balcony.

A point to bear in mind about crassulas is that many of them dramatically change leaf colour when stressed. In the cold of midwinter, or if they are underfed, they can change from the usual green to a vivid red. I had neglected a small pot of *C. anomala* with tiny torpedo-shaped leaves. I had not repotted, fed or even watered it, and it rewarded me by turning a vivid scarlet. It then decided to flower and put up wiry stems, each tipped with a long-lasting bobble of tiny, crowded white flowers which floated above the red leaves. It is hard to imagine any more striking sight.

Some crassulas look like other plants. There are crassulas that look like cotyledons, sedums, haworthias and mesembryanthemums. There are also many small hybrids with names such as 'Baby's Necklace' because the leaves are strung along the stem forming 'beads'. Others such as 'Pagoda Village' and 'Devils Horns' have leaves that overlap, forming beautiful chubby columns with textured surfaces. These small ornamental varieties are addictive, and a well-grown specimen that has piled up for many years is a great addition to any plant collection. The leaves of some small crassulas are so closely packed they should be kept out of the rain to prevent rotting. They are ideal for growing on balconies or in slightly sheltered places. If they become woody at the base, cut them off, allow to dry for a couple of days and replant.

For the garden, *C. capitella* 'Campfire' is a larger tumbler, worth seeking out. Its leaves are green in spring and a joyful, vivid, fall-red over winter. There are various cultivars sold as Propeller Plants (*C. perfoliata* var. *falcata*) which are good flowerers and

Crassula capitella 'Campfire' showing off its dramatic winter colouring, *Kalanchoe thyrsifolia* in front.

much loved by butterflies. *C. lycopodioides*, to 25 cm (10 in), has numerous tiny leaves which give an unexpectedly rough texture to its green spaghetti-like stalks, a good foil for more solid-leaved succulents. *C. streyi*, to about 30 cm (12 in), is an interesting species. Its green leaves have prominent purple spots, and the backs are a bright plum. It is hard to grow a perfect specimen of this particular crassula because its leaves seem vulnerable to insects, but it is magnificent as a garden plant, nibbles and all.

C. cordata is a neat small bush with grey-green leaves. It has spires of fairly inconspicuous flowers, each of which is surrounded by two soft green bracts, which results in a cloudy mass of long-lasting bracts that looks rather like a gypsophila. It is a great favourite, and is suitable for balconies as the flowers are held on fine, wiry, windproof stems.

Echeveria

Mexico, Central America. Rosette plants 3–50 cm (1ʺ–20 in) across. Amongst the most popular of all succulents, and a very varied and beautiful group. Echeverias need more food and more water than many other succulents. Highly decorative, they are superb landscaping plants in the garden and make the most beautiful specimens in pots. They grow fairly fast, which is always good. Echeverias can be divided broadly into species or near-species, and hybrids. The species and grey echeverias are on the whole tougher, smaller, can be grown in sun or shade, and often mound up into very attractive heaps. The hybrids are usually larger, are at their best in semi-shade, and often go brilliant colours in winter. The following is only a brief listing of some of the beautiful echeverias available.

Small species include *E. secunda*, 8 cm (3 in) across and high—an effective use of this plant is described in Chapter 7, Architectural Succulents—and the grey, neat, exquisite *E. elegans*, 8 cm (3 in) across; both are useful for massing. Echeverias to grow as specimens include *E. pallida*, a useful pale lime green, which grows into a small bush (one of the few echeverias enjoyed by snails); *E. minima* and *E. derenbergii*, both of which are tiny and neat; *E.*

Some echeverias colour brilliantly in winter, including, from left, 'Bittersweet', 'Alta May', 'Mauna Loa' and 'Mary Butterfield'; 'Fireball' is just visible.

prolifera, 8 cm (3 in) across, is small, grey and exuberant. *E. subsessilis*, 25 cm (10 in) across, is a gentle soft grey with a hint of pink.

All the hybrids are beautiful, but some of the most distinctive are: 'Perle von Nurnberg', 20 cm (8 in) across, a strong pink; 'Crinoline', 'Blue Curls', the typical 'lettuce' look; 'Princess Anne', pale green with lilac and peach shades when stressed; 'Pappy's Rose', a shiny mahogany; 'Lola', 15 cm (6 in) across, a pretty, neat, grey-green rosette with lovely lilac shading on the leaves, good for bedding. A single head of the pale violet 'Afterglow', 45 cm (18 in) across, looks as

Echeveria fasciculata, large, shiny and interesting.

dramatic as anything in the garden, rather like a pink agave. Beheaded, it sprouts many smaller heads. Grow it both ways for fun.

The large *E. fasciculata*, 50 cm (20 in) across, one of the most beautiful, is rich green with bronzy red tips to its leaves, it makes a spectacular, healthy and cheery specimen; the red seems to glow in the sun. 'Frank Renault' is an *E. agavoides* cultivar; the fat, wedge-shaped leaves have rose-pink tips that intensify when stressed or in winter. 'Paul Bunyan', 'Barbillion' and 'Cameo' are some of the carunculated varieties which have highly decorative, warty growths on their leaves.

Some echeverias do not show their full characteristics until they are mature. *E.* 'Mauna Loa' is one of these. It develops carunculations the length of its leaves only when mature, its second year onwards. Once it is in a 25 cm (10 in) pot, leave it alone and it should erupt like the volcano after which it is named. In winter it goes scarlet and purple and is a highly dramatic sight. You either love it or hate it. The flower stems are long, and the plant puts so much strength into them that it can temporarily lose the carunculations, so cut them off before they flower.

Echeveria 'Frank Renault': an agavoides type, which stresses pink in winter.

Many echeverias change colour in winter. 'Fireball' turns a vivid scarlet, and the edges of 'Big Red' turn red. Some of the curly-leaved ones, such as 'Alta May', 'Rosea Grande' and 'Mary Butterfield', colour beautifully in winter, too. They look greener but still interesting in summer.

Some echeverias have showy flowers: the shiny black 'Black Prince' has deep red flowers; *E. purpusorum*, *E. racemosa* and 'Gusto' are all fairly short-stemmed, vivid scarlet and yellow; *E. secunda* has pink and yellow flowers. 'Giant Mexican Firecracker', which grows loosely as a semi-shrub to 50 cm (20 in) has bright scarlet flowers in late winter. Not to be confused with it is 'Mexican Giant', which is large, silvery, a soft luminous white warmed by a baby-pink flush.

Many echeverias offset, producing small plants at the base. If left alone these form neat mats, but they can be divided at any time of the year. Others, mainly the hybrids, develop a tall, often decorative stem, which when it gets too long will need beheading.

Echeverias flower at different times of the year, the long flower stalks uncurling gradually, so there is nearly always one in flower. Echeverias respond to different growing conditions quite dramatically. Grown soft, with fertiliser and a bit of compost, they will grow four times bigger than if grown hard.

Euphorbia

Africa through to India. The most diverse of all succulent genera. They are pest free, partly because their sap is highly toxic, but not all euphorbias are succulent (*E. mysinites*, *E. cyparissias*, *E. rigida* and *E. wulfenii* are useful low-water non-succulent garden varieties). Succulent euphorbias are very varied, some growing as large as trees, like *E. grandidens*, with strappy leaves borne like candelabra. Others have reduced their leaves to spines, and can be confused with cacti, such as *E. grandicornis*, of which there are variegated kinds, and *E. heptagona*; both grow to 1 m (3 ft).

E. caput-medusae (Medusa's Head) is strange but decorative, with curving cylindrical branches radiating out from a central growth point. In the garden it looks like a neat bunch of octopus tentacles, anything from 30 cm (12 in) long. When suited it can grow to a pile 1.5 m (5 ft) wide and 1 m (3 ft) high, looking like an imaginatively iced cake. Quite a sight, especially when the flowers sprinkle the ends of the 'tentacles'. If you intend it to grow big, it is essential to plant it correctly in the beginning, on top of a mound. As it gets bigger, it can weigh itself down, and it is essential that its base does not become damp, as it can rot. Sprinkle snail bait in wet weather. In a pot the same plant grows long, sags with age and definitely looks like Medusa with a head full of snakes.

E. trigona is a good choice if you want a cactus effect in a tropical climate which is too humid for cacti. In cool climates the stems turn a beautiful maroon red; if frost touches the tips or if you wish to make the plant grow bushier, cut off the tips, and it will sprout further 'pipes'. It makes a spectacular upright cactus-like plant with little leaves sticking out at right angles from the trunk.

There are many collector's euphorbias, such as *E. obesa*, that appreciate the shelter of a shadehouse to grow unblemished, but I have seen them look pretty good in the garden too. Some have wonderful shapes, like the hats of Catholic clerics. You can stand looking at them, and hope you will never lose the ability to be struck dumb with admiration that the plant world has devised so many extraordinary ways of *being*.

Euphorbia flowers are usually inconspicuous. It is the bracts surrounding them that are decorative, not to say dramatic, as in the case of Poinsettia, *E. pulcherrima*, 3 m (10 ft), which is one of the larger members of the group. *E. milii* grows to a prickly bush about 1.5 m (5 ft) wide to 1 m (3 ft) high, covered the whole year with small, vivid red bracts. For anyone with a dog problem, this is prickly enough to be a deterrent. Recently, many pretty hybrids of *E. milii*—dainty red and yellow and cream, and small enough to be pot-friendly—have been introduced. They are scarcely ever without the vivid bracts that cover the whole bush.

Care should always be taken when handling euphorbias, as the sticky white sap of some kinds is highly allergenic, in some cases carcinogenic. Never let the sap get in your eyes, it can sting badly, even cause blindness. Remember to rinse euphorbia cuttings under a tap until the sap stops flowing.

Graptopetalum

Mexico. 5 cm (2 in) across. A rosette genus with many interesting hybrids, very useful for borders and superb as container plants for hot places. Graptopetalums have starry flowers on short stalks. You would not grow one solely for the flowers, but they are pretty enough. After flowering the stalks are untidy but easy to snap off. One of the toughest of all succulents, brilliant in sun, semi-shade or frost, is *G. paraguayense*, a grey-white rosette which develops raspberry blotches in winter. As it grows the stems elongate to produce a graceful cascading effect which is very good for hanging baskets and rockeries, but if this is not desirable cut off the heads and re-root. Children love to take leaves off *G. paraguayense*, and watch as over a month they develop roots and then plantlets. *Graptopetalum* hybridises freely with *Echeveria* and the hybrids, called x *Graptoveria*, tend to be smallish, neat rosettes with variable appearances, to be sought out as treasures. They include 'Debbie', a strong pink rosette; 'White Nun', a neat silvery grey trailer; 'Fanfare', like small grey starbursts; and 'Margaret Reppin', a neat bluish clumper with a small point at the end of each leaf which gives it a starry appearance.

Haworthia

South Africa, Namibia. To 10 cm (4 in). There are literally thousands of these, all subtly different—some upright, some spreading, some with a division in the centre. Haworthia flowers are small white slippers at the end of long wiry stems, not showy, but ethereal and gently decorative. Haworthias are very useful as they grow well in shade, though some can take sun for a few hours a day. The variety is so enormous, it is necessary to generalise and divide them roughly into two main groups. The first group is hard to the touch, and they either curve inwards with beautifully stippled stripes on the backs of their dark leaves, or outwards with hard sandpapery surfaces which can glisten and twinkle. They are drought resistant and perfect in rockeries where they grow into clusters that look like a group of huddled grouse. After a few years they might need to be separated and spread out.

The second group is quite squashy, tend to be light green and shiny, and make you feel they would pop if you squeezed them. They photosynthesise through the glassy tops of their leaves, and prefer diffuse but still good light. These haworthias mound up into decorative piles and make good, clean and green shade or windowsill plants.

Kalanchoe

Africa, Madagascar, Yemen. A large genus, kalanchoes vary greatly in size and impact, and do as well in the ground as in a pot. Most are grown for their leaves, but some, such as the *K. blossfeldiana* hybrids, are grown for their pretty, long-lasting flowers. These hybrids have healthy-looking green or grey leaves and the flowers come in red, yellow and white. *K. pumila*, a particularly pretty species, has grey leaves with sugar-pink flowers.

Kalanchoes are especially good for dry corners, being drought tolerant and untempting to snails. They can be broadly divided into two sorts: felted and waxy leaved. Some of the felted kinds have the largest and most dramatic leaves. *K. beharensis*, the largest of them all, has leaves shaped like a huge triangle up to 50 cm (20 in) long. The leaves begin a soft, hairy, apple green, but as they age the hairs turn brown and the leaves reflex (turn back) until they point to the ground, like an enormously graceful, if elephantine, ballet dancer. (It has been called 'Dripper', which is another way of looking at it.) I have seen this growing on a sand belt, sweltering in the humid 40°C (104°F) heat of Fremantle, Western Australia, 2 m (7 ft) high and 5 m (17 ft) wide. Stunning. Sometimes the judicious removal of inward-growing branches is necessary. 'Fangs' (see Chapter 12, Mod, Mad and Marvellous) is a *K. beharensis* cultivar with

The soft blue leaves of *Kalanchoe fedtschenkoi* almost submerged by sedum flowers.

Kalanchoe peltata, in a pot with *Echeveria derenbergii*, a trailing graptoveria and a touch of black mondo grass.

extraordinary protuberances on the underside of its leaves.

There is a group of felted kalanchoes called 'oak leaved' because of the lobed shape of their leaves. They reach 1–2 m (3–7 ft) and are worth searching for as they are particularly good as backdrop plants. In the wild they grow where they can capture moisture from mists or dew. Good in pots or in the ground, they are easy to grow from cuttings or leaves. Cut back after flowering.

K. peltata, which grows like a small bush to 75 cm (30 in), is amongst the whitest plants in the garden. Its leaves are a velvety matt white and held upright like little flags. It is a good specimen plant, and similar in garden value to a miniature conifer. It is tough and sends out a web of fine, brown, aerial roots which are decorative as they stream downwards either into the earth or over the edge of a pot.

Particularly beautiful, drought tolerant and

underused is *K. fedtschenkoi*, a small bush to 40 cm (16 in) with bluish leaves which look luminous in the twilight, a beautiful sight. (Suggestions for using it appear in Chapter 4.) *K. thyrsifolia* has recently become widely available (sold as 'Flapjacks'). It has large, paddle-like leaves with a distinct red flush round the rim, especially if grown in full sun. It is a statuesque, slow-growing and garden-worthy plant.

K. delagoensis (syns *K. tubiflora*, *Bryophyllum verticillatum*) has a decorative, attractive and long-lasting mop of tubular salmon flowers on a stem 1 m (3 ft) high. I love to watch the great honeyeaters swaying on the stem probing each flower for nectar with their long, curved beaks. The little plantlets growing on the edges of the leaves, however, make it a dangerous addition to rural gardens and gardens adjoining bushland, as it becomes a pest if it escapes into the wild.

Sedum

Asia, Europe, North Africa, North America. 5–30 cm (2–12 in). An easy, decorative and varied genus with more than 600 members. It is hard to generalise about sedums, but any that are offered for sale will be garden worthy. Some are evergreen, some are herbaceous. *S. rubrotinctum*, *S. pachyphyllum* and *S. allantoides* have colourful jellybean-shaped leaves. *S. furfuraceum*, up to 5 cm (2 in) high and 20 cm (8 in) across, its fat leaves green with red shadows, is a slow, small mounder. *S. mexicanum*, a finely leaved tumbler—try to find the pretty golden version—needs better food and more water than some of the other tougher sedums. *S. acre* is tiny, slightly larger that a

Sedum burrito used as a houseplant in Mathew Brennan's sunny living room.

obtain it again, but it had seeded, and I was left with a hybrid, nearly as dark, slightly larger. A beautiful thing. Someone, somewhere, might have the original for sale, and it is worth keeping an eye out for such curiosities.

Agapanthus seeds are heavy, and whatever mechanism exists in their natural habitat for scattering seeds does not operate under my conditions; the seed always drops near or downhill of a plant. So if you want them to spread, pick off the seeds, which persist a long time on the seed head, and scatter them—but please, if you live next to bush, don't allow your agapanthus to escape into the wild.

moss, with minute yellow flowers. *S. spathulifolium* is a popular, tough, grey carpeter, and *S. allantoides* has small, finger-like leaves of a piercing lime green. I grow this in a small pot, its pale green a wonderful contrast against the very dark green of a creeping ficus. It is tough. Pale green *S. morganianum* (Donkey's Tails), is popular for hanging baskets. It trails downwards for 1 m (3 ft). Trim sedums after flowering.

Companion bulb: *Agapanthus*

South Africa. 30 cm–1 m (12 in–3 ft). Large, mop-headed blue and white agapanthus are so common at the height of summer it is easy to take them for granted, but what survivors they are. There are also several rare varieties to look out for. I find the ones said to be pink bleach very quickly. Years ago I had one that was an inky dark blue. Unlike the ordinary agapanthus which holds each floret facing outwards, the bells drooped heavily. The whole head, though on a 1.5 m (5 ft) stalk, was not large, but it was of such an intense indigo blue that it had a powerful presence in the bush garden I grew it in. Someone stole it. I confess to savage thoughts about such bandits. I was not able to

A dramatic flowering of agapanthus with a variegated flax and *Echeveria secunda*'s dizzy mass of dried flower stalks in the foreground.

4 Gardens and Courtyards

My top ten

Aeonium arboreum 'Zwartkop'
Agave americana 'Mediopicta Alba'
Crassula capitella 'Campfire'
Echeveria 'Imbricata'
Kalanchoe peltata
Othonna capensis
Puya mirabilis
Sedum rubrotinctum
Senecio serpens 'Blue Chalksticks'
Tradescantia (purple clone)
Companion bulb: *Sauromatum guttatum*

This chapter is about how to grow succulents in an average-sized garden or courtyard. Many have already been discussed, but here I hope you will find how to incorporate them into groups and garden schemes. Following chapters discuss using succulents in very small gardens, in miniature gardens and as landscape plants. The succulents in this chapter are of a middle size and tough, and are easy to accommodate in an average garden, but to add interest you can include larger plants from Chapter 7, Architectural Succulents, and smaller ones from Chapter 5, Small Gardens.

A low-water garden in a Mediterranean climate can be made using only succulents or cacti, or it can use succulents as part of a complex planting with other low-water plants. Many people think that plants that come from dry regions must *look* dry and less beautiful than their pampered cousins. But plants from low-water climates will actually look far more beautiful in a Mediterranean climate than plants from a high-rainfall climate struggling to survive in conditions for which they are not suited. A succulent garden is no different to any other, except that it needs less water, which is why succulents survive in difficult spots, and in the gardens of rarely visited holiday houses.

All successful gardens have a balance of shapes and textures, of mass and space. I describe some suggested plantings, but if a planting of succulents does not please, it is only a moment away from a change, as most can be easily dug up and moved.

If you are not familiar with succulents it can help to visualise them as the equivalents of more familiar plants. Many sedums have a 'mop' effect, *S. lydium* has the effect of alyssum, or Sweet Alice, *S. acre* the effect of a clump of moss. *Kalanchoe peltata* looks like a trimmed box—but white. Echeverias look like chunkier sempervivums, a cotyledon can have the effect in the garden of an artemisia, and *Kalanchoe fedtschenkoi* perhaps could be thought to have something of the effect of *Stachys lanata* (Lamb's Tongues). Aeoniums make 'bushes', but with strikingly bold leaves. Crassulas creep and tumble and, with the sedums, form 'cushions'.

To introduce succulents into a garden that you do

Flowering aeoniums and aloes add colour to Jimmie Morrison's colourful entrance

not want to change entirely, take a careful look at the existing planting. Watering systems come in sections, so choose one for your low-water garden in which the sprinklers can easily be turned off, or down. Make sure this section has good light—it can have some shade but not deep shade—and good drainage. Move your favourite high-water plants to another section where they can happily continue to grow together. If the soil is poor, add some compost to 'open up' the soil and help it to retain water, so that a little water will go a long way. If the garden bed needs better drainage add coarse river sand, or even pumice or perlite for a small area.

Succulents can be used like conventional plants, as clumpers, bushes, specimens and so on, but they are also superb when used in more contemporary ways, in minimalist swathes or disciplined blocks. There are suggestions for all types of plantings scattered through this chapter and also in Chapter 12, Mod, Mad and Marvellous. There are also more suggestions for pot plants in that chapter and in Chapter 1, Growing Succulents.

Aeonium arboreum 'Zwartkop'

Aeoniums are architectural subshrubs, some of which grow to 1 m (3 ft). They mound up in an interesting way, they survive in dry places, and you often see them flourishing in churchyards or beside the road. *Aeonium* 'Zwartkop'—inky black in full sun—is dramatic in blocks and drifts, and superb as a specimen plant. In the ground it grows to 50 cm (20 in) with expanded leaves giving it a shaggy look. If it has a restricted root run the black heads remain packed in tight rosettes. Grow these with grey plants, or make a black garden with black mondo grass and *Echeveria* 'Black Knight'. There are begonias and geraniums with near-black leaves too. Go wild.

Many small aeoniums are hidden in plant lists as 'unnamed species'. They are mostly drought tolerant with pretty, fresh green leaves and froths of yellow flowers. In summer they purse up to reduce evaporation. They can look so different you might feel you have two plants for the price of one. Plants like these are to be sought out and treasured.

My courtyard, with many succulents that look good all year round.

Agave americana 'Mediopicta'

Agaves are amongst the most architectural and beautiful of succulents. There are many varieties, and it is worth selecting carefully as they are hard to move when they get large. *A. americana* has many forms, two of which are 'Mediopicta Alba', a good, neat agave with strong white stripes and about 75 cm (30 in) across and high (incidentally, this is first recorded as being offered for sale in a Dutch nursery in 1714), and a version with yellow variegation which grows slightly larger. *A. victoria-reginae* makes a particularly successful, smaller feature plant, with neat striped leaves. *A. attenuata* has very beautiful soft leaves and is good beside pools and in other places where you do not want a plant with spines. *A. geminiflora*, again 75 cm (30 in) across, is a soft-leaved species with fine radiating leaves, smaller than a dasylirion and larger than *A. stricta*, which is 30 cm (12 in) across. Agaves produce 'pups' and it is a good idea once a year to put on stout gloves and pull these gently away, as these plants look less dramatic as a cluster. Most agaves will flourish in pots.

Strong foliage; the striking *Agave americana* 'Medio-picta alba' is on the right.

The very similar aloes, from southern Africa, have larger roots than agaves and although they can be grown in containers, you might need to trim their roots occasionally when you repot them. Aloe leaves are softer than those of agaves on the whole. *Aloe striata* has a dramatic impact in a mixed planting, with its pale green, boat-shaped leaves which are striped along their length with a delightful pink edge; it tolerates a wide range of conditions.

Crassula capitella 'Campfire'

This has long, leafed stems that trail in a useful way for tall pots or rockeries (I grow one tumbling out of an old chimney pot). It is a thoroughly pleasant plant, but it positively stars in winter, when the leaves, a lovely fresh green in summer, turn a vivid scarlet. The scarlet fades slowly in early summer, becoming green, though the red edging persists for quite a time. The flowers, small and white, are delicious too. Nothing is nicer in your own garden than to have a few plants that look remarkably different at certain seasons. Trim to neaten if necessary, remembering, that like all crassulas, the smallest bit will strike. In all the years I have treasured this it has never once looked limp; it would be ideal tumbling from the top of a retaining wall. The scarlet of the winter 'Campfire' would look superb against purple tradescantia (see below) or grey-leaved plants.

Echeveria 'Imbricata'

Frequently seen simply because it does well, often naturalising in a Mediterranean climate, and enduring frost and drought, *Echeveria* 'Imbricata' is a large blue-grey rosette to 25 cm (10 in) across, with a pink flush on the ends of its leaves. It is superb when used as a repetitive motif, such as a border. It may cluster in time, and if you prefer to grow it as a specimen simply detach the pups. You may occasionally need to behead it and replant to keep it neat.

Kalanchoe peltata

The neat tear-shaped bush of the white-leaved *Kalanchoe peltata* provides a geometric accent perhaps against a sea of soft blue *K. fedtschenkoi*. A row of the pink rosettes of *Graptoveria* 'Debbie' would be pretty in front of it. These are plants that need little water. Both *Kalanchoe fedtschenkoi* and *K. peltata* need to be grown hard, so plant them in good free-draining soil with a bit of cow manure; too little water will make them look tired, but the occasional watering will keep them compact and beautiful. *K. marmorata* is a larger-leaved species, unusual and strong, which gets to about 40 cm (16 in) high. Grown hard, it has striking brown spots on the leaves. Again, cut it back if it becomes lank.

A dry bank landscaped with a pink-leaved kalanchoe between grey cotyledons and an agave.

Othonna capensis

This is a strange-looking little plant. It is made up of small juicy segments about the size of gelatine medication capsules, though it is a bit 'Morse code'— some are long and some are short. For most of the year its little yellow daisy flowers bounce gaily above the green. I find that this simple plant gets more than its fair share of admirers. I grow it in a plastic pot wedged inside a pottery bread bin which has a beautiful mahogany glaze; it tumbles down the sides looking fresh and bright. It would do well in a hanging basket, over a rock (it roots as it goes), or as a trailer in a steep place.

Puya mirabilis

There are many puyas (native to Argentina and Bolivia), which are good for well-drained hot places. Their fine puffballs provide a strong accent and are good for landscaping. Some puyas are silvery thistle-

Othonna capensis, an interesting small tumbler.

bursts of foliage, others are hook-edged, starry and bushy. Some have the most beautiful flowers it is possible to imagine. *P. mirabilis* has dramatic green flowers, *P. alpestris* has flowers of viridian green, electric blue, vastly tall. *P. venusta* has dramatic red and purple flowers. If you made a film about another world, puyas would be amongst the plants you would choose to show you were not on planet Earth. They contrast well with the tubby shapes of cacti, but do not seem to transplant very well, so perhaps it is best to acquire them small.

Sedum rubrotinctum

Sedums are easy, and form mop-like cushions. There are many forms, lush green, variegated, glaucous. Some are evergreen, others die down each year. Sedums slowly form neat attractive mounds over winter, only to shock in spring when over a three-week period they explode into growth, still neat, still nice but … bigger. The flowers are frothy, usually white or yellow. Trim them if you want them neater, but their exuberance is part of their charm. *S. rubrotinctum* 'Jelly Beans', from Mexico, has many varieties; 'Aurora', a pale pink, is pretty; grow it hard in diffuse

Urns of *Echeveria elegans* and cotyledon in Susie Mann's garden stand out against a froth of blue echiums and yellow-flowering sedums.

light to get the best colours. *S. roseum* is a lovely small purple spreader. *S. pachyphyllum* takes full sun, it is grey with red tips. Plants that mound are useful in a garden.

Most plectranthus need shade and water, but there is a small succulent species, *Plectranthus caeruleus*, which has small, furry, grey aromatic leaves, with violet shadows in winter. Its brittle growth is so higgledy-piggledy that it looks as if it could be used to demonstrate the chaos theory single-handed. It has a curious quality—when its branches cross they sometimes fuse together. It has the same garden value as catmint, also a low-water plant, but it does not have catmint's unpleasant smell or popularity with cats.

Senecio serpens

Senecio serpens is a good edger and groundcover; tough, it creeps to form a mat. It glows blue, so plant it in front of yellow *Sedum nussbaumerianum* (no fertiliser for best colour) or anything grey to add a note of drama to the garden. Drosanthemums and lampranthuses, which are good companions, are covered in flowers in spring. But the real garden power of a lampranthus lies in the paired grey-green leaves which lie on either side of a lax violet stem. It is not only beautiful, but the neat tumble looks good the whole year round.

Tradescantia

The purple-leaved clone of *Tradescantia* provides an impressive accent in the garden or in pots with its strongly coloured leaves. Grow it against an orange wall or in front of grey plants. The tiny pink, starry flowers only add to its beauty. Remember to water it occasionally—like all tough plants it is easy to forget to water it and the leaves then curl in upon themselves and look a bit dusty.

Companion bulb: *Sauromatum guttatum*

70 cm (28 in). A member of the Araceae, or Arum, family, this is actually a corm rather than a bulb. It is not often grown, but I find it has a particularly strong impact in a mixed planting. I treasure it for its single huge, lobed leaf, rather like a palm frond, which grows on a tall stem covered in decorative purple blotches. The corm, the size of a saucer, makes a striking

The interesting leaf of *Sauromatum guttatum*.

decoration if you dig one up at the end of winter, and put it inside, unwatered, on a plate. It slowly develops a spike 40 cm (16 in) high which turns into a striking, monstrous, deep maroon arum-like flower. The flower will only last a few days, and you can then plant the corm out again.

The new Getty Museum in Los Angeles had an impressive concept for the inaugural planting of its garden. A hill was planted using plants from high to low altitudes. Many succulents come from high altitudes where the air is dryer, so the top half of the garden was an anthology of dry-country plants, and a path wound down to the bottom to lush swampland plants from the better-watered coastal plains. Memorable were the ranks of *Echeveria* 'Lola' (a Dick Wright hybrid) as large as grapefruit, pale celadon grey with violet shadows (see page 82). 'Lola' offsets, but slowly, and so is useful if you want to achieve a relatively static planting.

One person's problem garden can be another person's treasure. Netzia van Eeten, a succulent lover, purchased a house in Melbourne with a garden which dropped precipitously from the house to a retaining wall standing at chest height above the pavement. Small pockets of earth and high drainage. It was perfect for succulents. Within eighteen months it had taken on a settled air. Many succulents had been brought from her previous garden in pots and had responded

Echeveria glauca and *elegans*, aeoniums, cotyledons and kalanchoes make a beautiful and trouble free planting for a bank in Sue and Tony Darvall's garden.

enthusiastically to being planted on the hot slope. Height was given to the planting with several small trees including the small *Cussonia spicata*, 2 m (7 ft). Cussonias have fresh, highly lobed, grey-green leaves on long stalks which spring from the crown rather like palm fronds and then reflex so that the head is nearly spherical. New fronds glow pinkish in spring, and this little tree casts a pretty shadow, making it doubly decorative. Strong-shaped cacti and succulents were planted in blocks with finer-leaved succulents in between.

The problems were unexpected—the garden looked so pretty from the road that inquisitive or, rather, *acquisitive* fingers pinched everything within reach. This was cleverly solved by taking out the soft, succulent tumblers and planting the prickliest, most tenacious plants in a phalanx along the pavement— prickly cacti, spiny and thorny euphorbias. This garden is a textbook of the rare, the extraordinary and the enviable. I wonder it has not caused accidents as cars round the corner.

My own garden is mostly low water except for a small vegetable patch where I grow herbs, lettuces and tomatoes. I have a large sunny courtyard where there are many succulents in pots against a perimeter planting of gardenias and camellias. The area is unified by the shiny green foliage of *Veltheimia* (described in Chapter 10, Shady Characters), a bulb whose foliage is a perfect foil for the succulents. There is a side path where there is room for a table, in the filtered light from a neighbour's trees, upon which to keep small plants so they can be checked, and this together with a metal bookcase forms my nursery, infirmary and a parking lot for spares.

The back garden, which is about the size of a tennis court, has old camellia trees which make a good neutral backdrop, especially if clipped. They need some water in summer, and the little they get is sufficient to support a *Mahonia lomarifolia* with its primitive holly-like leaves, crinums and arums and other strange Araceae. There are two specimens of the versatile shrub *Viburnum macrocephalum*, one growing happily in dry shade, the other in hot sun, with white 'snowball' flowers twice a year, in spring and autumn. This double flowering is very welcome in a small garden. I planted

Iris foetidissima for its wonderful seedpods, and bulbs—hymenocallis, crinums, red sprekelia, galtonia—that need (and get) little water. A succulent parterre (see Chapter 13, Designing with Succulents) also gives me much pleasure.

Over the years I have pocketed the odd interesting stone. From the Caspian Sea, from a wedding held on the flood-banks of a river. Beach walks over the years have yielded treasures—a strange dough-coloured sea-worn rock like a smooth tube that pleased me, and a fine-grained grey disc with a dip in the middle where a fossil had lain. In my life these are not just stones, to me they are *stepping* stones, each with a memory. They live in my garden where I can see them, they are useful to hold down a plant prone to blowing over, they act as a mulch over a small root, and in a tiny garden they can masquerade as a boulder.

We mostly garden alone, and a loved garden can take on the role of a valued companion, applauding our efforts by looking spectacular, or gently pointing out what we have overlooked. A garden should have a personality. It should echo its owner, it should have personal touches, and show preferences and prejudices. It should have mistakes and vision. It can have the occasional gap where something has died. A good garden, in short, is a perfect metaphor for life.

Echeveria 'Lola', with graptoveria growing through the holes in a tall pot with a topknot of *Carex* 'Curly Locks'.

5 Small Gardens

My top ten
Agave stricta
Asparagus 'Cats' Tails'
Crassula
Echeveria globulosa
Gasteria
Haworthia
Opuntia species (miniatures)
Sedum lydium
Pachypodium geayi
Peperomia columella
Companion bulb: *Ferraria crispa*

Small areas usually have constraints other than just size. They may have limited sun, poor soil, and will almost certainly be drier than is ideal—roofs overhang and the earth always seems to be dry near walls. These conditions can often be perfect for *carefully selected* succulents and scree-dwellers that are highly tolerant of difficult conditions. The beauty of a garden has very little to do with size but everything to do with its structure, where scale and texture are controlled so that the components achieve a balance. Enormous fun and satisfaction can be had from an area that at first might seem to have limited potential. There are many small succulents that are terrific to 'furnish' a low-water garden; their strong shapes preventing a small area being 'mimsy', or looking weak and ineffectual.

Victor Aprozeanu's small corner landscaped with succulents.

Agave stricta

There are many small agaves, aloes and cacti which are most useful to help form an architectural framework. The thin spiny leaves of *Agave stricta*, from Mexico, radiate out to form a neat football-sized puff of green. It is one of the most underused of all aloes. It is pretty, a good green, and makes a superb contrast plant for a small garden.

Echeveria, sedums, crassula and cactus surround a tiny pond.

Asparagus 'Cats' Tails'

Asparagus are hardy and make very pretty, fresh green bushes or climbers with clouds of fresh green, tiny needle-like leaves over summer. *A.densiflorus sarmentosa* 'Cats' Tails' makes a small evergreen bush with leaves arranged in spiral whorls up the stem forming 'tails'. This is very tough. *A. densiflorus sprengeri* is a non-succulent but billowing variety to 1 m (3 ft). They both bear attractive red berries in autumn which make for pretty picking; cut them off anyway as they can seed. Asparagus are not always easy to find, but are well worth keeping an eye out for.

Crassula

There are many varieties of crassulas and sedums which form neat and pretty heaps and drifts, some of them having extended flowering seasons. They are easy to keep tidy, with a trim if necessary. Many of them have been described in previous chapters.

Echeveria elegans

Perhaps the neatest and prettiest echeveria for massing, *E. elegans* is the palest grey, slightly cupped. It offsets, but not as freely as *E. secunda* or *E. glauca*. If they are grown in full sun they will need occasional watering over hot periods.

Kalanchoe thyrsifolia on the left, with *Asparagus* 'Cats' Tails' in the swan, *Aloe striata* in front.

Gasteria

Tall, stumpy, spotted, plain, dark or shiny—there are many gasterias, and they have the added advantage, remember, that they are good in rooty places under trees (see Chapter 9, Shady Characters).

Haworthia

Rosette plants, again with a vast number of varieties which are good in shady places (see Chapter 3, Most Popular and Easily Grown; Chapter 9, Shady Characters).

Opuntia

Cacti can be green or white or even hairy, and are superb especially in areas of great heat, where a garden of *Trichocereus* will provide as much colour for nearly as long as a rose garden. Opuntias are cacti ranging from tree-size to miniatures, and they are strikingly decorative with their flat, paddle-like leaves. Some have flat small pads, often covered with white or gold tufts of either spines or hairs. Some have very round leaves, others quite elongated pads, some are decidedly tear-shaped. Opuntias are useful where you need a strong outline (see Chapter 4, Most Popular and Easily Grown, for more about cacti).

Pachypodium geayi

Pachypodium geayi and *P. lamerei* are small trees from Madagascar or Namibia, which look like small palms with a trunk covered with spines and foliage sprouting from the top. They are very attractive and dramatic container plants for a sheltered patio or conservatory,

The visual appeal of a plant with spines, such as this opuntia, benefits from backlighting.

but make sure the container is a deep one, as they have a long taproot.

P. geayi is a superbly sculptural succulent, its 1.5 m (5 ft) trunk bristling with spines and little fronds spraying out of the top like a small palm tree. Unusual and intriguing, it has a tree presence.

Pachypodium geayi makes a dramatic statement by a doorway.

Peperomia columella

For shade and sheltered places think of the highly architectural peperomias—some have round leaves, often with pretty stripes or patterns. *P. columella*, which has oval 'windows' like portholes up its columnar stems, and gasterias are good for sheltered places where you need something interesting.

Sedum lydium

Try *S. lydium* for a green tumble, or *S. spathulifolium* for a pretty grey bobbly look.

Companion bulb: *Ferraria crispa*

South Africa. A small bulb, really a corm, to 20 cm (8 in) high. The flowers are like small black starfish that have been dusted with gold; there are yellow and khaki versions as well. I put some compost through an old sandpit, planted a few bulbs and a thicket developed in a few years. It is good for difficult dry places because it never needs watering—it grows in winter when there is enough rain and is dormant in summer. The flowers come out over a long period. Although it does not last long when picked, it makes a strange and unusual addition to a posy, and to a garden.

I would love to tell you about two favourite small gardens I know that make very effective use of succulents.

Aprozeanu garden

Victor and Cristina Aprozeanu are serious low-water plant collectors; they have collections of succulents, cacti, bromeliads and Australian natives, all incorporated into their overall garden design. Victor loves exploring the new. Space is not wasted on familiar plants or spares, and if he gets bored with a plant he does not hesitate to pass it on. Space is also maximised by selecting small and slow-growing plants. Most of the plants have a story to tell, and tracking them down to the gardens of other keen collectors has been the starting point for many friendships.

The front garden is a well-drained slope with curving beds where there is room for a few larger plants. *Aloe ferox*, for instance, with its fiercely toothed leaves and scarlet flowers, is backed by neat gasterias, each carefully placed against a stone, the plainness of which acts as a foil for their dramatic 'fingers'. There are various succulent trees, the Australian *Brachychiton rupestris,* a *Chorisia insignis* from South America (recently renamed *Ceiba insignis*), its trunk studded with thorns, and the small *Cussonia spicata* with its mop of fresh leaves.

The front porch has a magnificently grown *Pachypodium geayi*, placed so that it gets maximum sun and shades the bromeliads behind it. The baffled light is perfect for bromeliads from South American rainforests, and there are also hanging baskets with unusual succulent trailers: *Ceropegia amplicata*, a bobbly *Senecio rowleyanus* and a strange, trailing fern, *Huperzia nummularifolia.*

Perhaps the most beautiful part of the garden is at the back of the house. The proportions of this small planting of sedums, aeoniums and crassulas are so perfect that it comes as a shock when standing in it to realise that it measures only 2 x 3 m (7 x 10 ft). The scale is set by a statue about 70 cm (28 in) high, with a ferny asparagus (*A. densiflorus sprengeri*) that looks like a Japanese pine in miniature billowing behind it. There are many species of asparagus which remain evergreen in a Mediterranean climate, and new shoots are always replacing the old. The 'shrubbery' is a tiny clumping crassula and the small *Sedum lydium.* Around the tiny pond—30 cm (12 in) square—rosettes of grey *Echeveria elegans* echo the carefully arranged surrounding grey stones, making the pond look much bigger than it is. A clump of *Ledebouria violacea* stands like small exclamation marks, with their

Three trailers, *Ceropegia amplicata*, the fern-like *Huperzia nummularifollia* and the bobbly *Senecio rowleyanus*, thrive in dappled light in the Aprozeanus' entrance.

Rita Brown's fantasy garden: the Spanish Mission Church landscaped with tiny crassulas, cacti, ledebourias and prickly pear to right and front.

beautiful plum-coloured leaves held upright. The only plant in this back garden that requires a lot of water is a papyrus. Growing in the pond, not only does it give height to the garden, but is cleverly placed so that at the end of the day its filmy head remains illuminated by the last rays of the sun.

A striking feature of this garden is how neat it is. Cacti and succulents are planted in enough soil for them to thrive, but they leave no nutrients or water for weeds, so it is in effect a low-maintenance garden. Apart from a small area of grass, the garden needs little watering. There is a lot to learn from this garden. It is a model for dry-country, low-maintenance gardening, but its success is due to the Aprozeanus' deep knowledge of their plants.

A garden for grandchildren

Rita Brown is an artist who has created a fairytale garden to share with her grandchildren. It is one of many 'rooms' in a larger garden: there is a 'King and

I' tropical pool with lotus and goldfish, a pair of iron high-heeled shoes filled with sempervivums stands on a chamomile lawn that leads to a leafy 'gnomery', and a stupendous vegetable garden. But the most special room in this garden begins at a white wrought-iron fence. This is not a utilitarian keep-the-dog-out-type of fence—the uprights are curved, reminiscent of a Spanish balcony—it is a fence that denotes a magic world. And every child knows that a fence has to have a gate, in this case a pair of rain-washed Indian doors with a lintel carved with elephants. It is only when you open the gate that you can enter the tiny magic world beyond.

Rita has collected or, rather, invited, inhabitants from all over the world, including Fairyland, to live in the world she has created. Only 3 m (10 ft) square, it is like a little village, each character having its own house and garden. Rita has made the buildings from pieces of wood and painted them in happy colours. There is an English farm with fields and fences, animals and gates; and a vegetable garden complete with the farmer's dwelling and rows of little china vegetables. Jack 's house at the foot of the Beanstalk is thatched with pluckings from a brush fence, his garden is shaded by a striking 'tree' (a jade plant made from carved amethysts), and green and grey santolinas and miniature conifers, all kept small by pruning.

Beans grow at Jack's back door, just where his mother threw them out, and Jack is swinging from the vine above, a scarlet runner bean, which is perennial, and has scarlet flowers, and beans you can pick, though in winter dizzy green modelling-clay beans hang from its dry stems. The giant lives on a tiny window-ledge, conveniently (for Rita and for the giant) high up in the air. He is surrounded by—what else?—'air plants', tillandsias, and has a horrid smile as he wields a hammer on the shoes he is making. A small child could equally well assume the smile is horrid and gleeful in anticipation of Jack's imminent arrival.

An Aussie house has chairs on the verandah, water tanks out the back and a row of crows on a white picket fence. There is a heavily populated Asian garden with water buffaloes toiling in a lake, and a battlemented castle in which a princess awaits her rescuer. He is, apparently, a white knight, but if he doesn't hurry up he could well be pipped at the post by the strapping young Jack hovering overhead.

A path winds up a hill past a pair of tiny lonicera arches to a Spanish mission church. The path is made from a sheet of doll's house bricks and the desert from the dust left over from laying a tennis court. It is hard to imagine anything more magical than the piazza in front of the church with a complicated design made from bonsai sand. It has some miniature cacti to make it feel at home. The miniature *Opuntia* cactus is obvious, there is a pair of cacti with white hairs swirling round, and others are in fact tiny spined euphorbias and *Monadenium ellenbeckii* masquerading as organ cactus. A cactus-looking euphorbia is easier to manage than a true cactus in this garden and besides, goodness knows what the fairy godmother night have done to it in the night! There are tiny upright crassulas, haworthias and a *Ledebouria violacea* makes a fine cycad (in Fairyland nothing is quite what it seems) with its upstanding purple-backed leaves. Rita used trimmings from a lonicera hedge elsewhere in the garden to make the tiny hedges, and the whole has been colonised by a tough green moss, accidentally introduced from a nursery—grass which never needs mowing.

This grandmother has five grandsons who love the garden. She has just got her first granddaughter—may she love it just as much. It seems like the perfect ending for a fairy tale.

6 Miniature Gardens and Balconies

My top ten

Agave stricta nana
Crassula (many small varieties and hybrids, including 'Damsel', 'Frosty', 'Jade Necklace', 'Pastel')
Echeveria minima
Gasteria bicolor var. *liliputana* ('Lilliput')
Monanthes polyphylla
Neohenricia sibbettii
Sedum acre
Sempervivum arachnoideum
Stomatium fulleri
Titanopsis calcarea
Companion bulb: *Ledebouria violacea*

In Mediterranean climates care has to be taken in small plantings to use plants that will not die if subjected to hot weather, and for this succulents are an ideal choice. A miniature garden is made up of many tiny plants grown together to make a landscape in a pot or a bowl which can be small enough to sit on a table. Such a garden can give hours of pleasure to someone who enjoys creating and 'fiddling' with something, or who misses a much-loved larger garden. Although I have succeeded in selecting plants for such arrangements that survive and look good in full sun, often, because there is so little soil to hold water, plantings such as these will do best with a little shade or shelter. One of the great joys of succulents is that they can be dug up and replanted so that you can make a completely different garden using the very same plants when you have become bored with the current arrangement. All the succulents listed in this chapter also have interesting flowers.

Miniature gardens or beautifully groomed specimen plants add style and pleasure to balconies and shaded growing spaces. A miniature garden has a jewel-like quality that is possessed by no other garden, an Alice-in-Wonderland feel that it just *might* be inhabited by spirits. I think there is a very good reason for this. In a large garden any plant, however loved, is almost always part of an overall tapestry. In a miniature garden everything is seen close up, every pore counts, the way each leaf sits on a stem matters, and every minute flower is a miracle. As long as a balcony or patio has room for a chair or two, and a table, it will have enough room for a miniature garden.

Agave stricta nana

This is a puffball of foliage, about the size of an orange, 10 cm (4 in) high and wide, with yellow leaves. A good accent plant. Do not confuse with *A. stricta* which is green, also beautiful and 30 cm (12 in), high and wide.

There are also many lovely small aloes I have mentioned elsewhere. *Aloe* 'Purple Shark', about

Agave stricta nana. The pot is just 12 cm (5 in) high

Crassula 'Jade Necklace'.

7 cm (2∫ in)across, is new in my garden and seems to be shaping up well. It has dark, finely toothed leaves which are a great foil for a variegated or pale-leaved succulent such as a small crassula.

Crassula 'Pastel'

This has fine, variegated, upright columns and provides a clean, fresh note in a mixed planting. There are many tiny crassulas: 'Damsel' is small and starry, 'Frosty' has fine hairs that make it look … frosty. 'Jade Necklace', with pretty, pink-edged triangular leaves … there are endless varieties with more or less upright growth. Crassulas and sedums are both grateful for any care and tolerant of less than ideal conditions.

Echeveria minima

The smallest of the echeverias, each of its rosettes being about as big as a thumbnail. This does not like to be dried out, but is delicious if cared for. For hotter situations *E. derenbergii* is the size of a small tangerine and tougher. It is celadon grey with tiny pink tips, very pretty.

Gasteria bicolor var. *liliputana* ('Lilliput')

The fat, fleshy leaves of this are smaller than a thumb knuckle. It does not like the onslaught of full sun, but is very happy in shaded situations; it spreads into a dear little tussock. There are many low-growing gasterias that can be used in small gardens.

For a hot position, try *Pleiospilos simulans*, which has a pair of fleshy, heavily keeled leaves reminiscent of a wide-open serpent's jaws, each 7 x 3 cm (2∫ x 1˜ in) with a texture like sharkskin, and bright shaggy yellow flowers sprouting from the centre. The leaves look something like a cross between a gasteria and a lithops, and it basks in full sun. Don't be alarmed if the leaves suddenly peel back in a cardboardy crumple, as two new ones will almost immediately poke through from the base of each old leaf. Oddities such as this

Pleiospilos simulans, snake-like, survives the hottest sun. New leaves are appearing in the centre.

can provide immense satisfaction. And for really hot places, a selection of lithops set against carefully selected gravel is hard to beat, always providing they can be kept dry when they need to be dormant after flowering.

Monanthes polyphylla

The small bobbles of tightly packed leaves of this plant spread to make a most beautiful fresh green mat. Its flowers are not very distinguished, but they are held on wiry 4 cm (1° in) stalks which have long-lasting bracts. This is a very pretty addition to a miniature planting and spreads fast, so will soon give you plenty to swap.

Neohenricia sibbettii

A small clumping succulent which forms a moss-like mat made up of tiny bobbles each of which looks like a tiny lithops. If stressed these become a soft donkey-brown suede colour.

Sedum acre

Sedums add a fresh note to succulent plantings. Their leaves are decorative as a mass rather than individually. *Sedum acre* is neat and nice; its soft undulating billow a good foil for more architectural succulents.

Sempervivum arachnoideum

Sempervivums need to be out of the full sun, but *S. arachnoideum* spins a pretty, webby, spidery presence. It is particularly good if nestled into something. If you

have an exceedingly hot garden, use the tiny cactus *Mammilaria gracilis*, which is hairy and bobbly and has a similar effect.

Stomatium fulleri

This has small, toothed leaves and looks like a small faucaria. It clumps up quite quickly, good for the impatient, and has white flowers which bunch at the end of long stems

Titanopsis calcarea

The grey-green kite-shaped leaves of this little plant have a frosting of fine pink spots on the ends, so that the tips of the leaves look as if they are made of lace; it also has a pretty flower.

Companion bulb: *Ledebouria violacea*

Southern Africa. 5 cm (2 in). There are also some larger species to 10 cm (4 in). The bulbs sit on top of the earth and cluster attractively. The grey-green leaves with white markings on the upper surface have purple backs. The flowers are a neat purple spire in early summer.

Find a container you really love, remembering that it will be heavier when filled with soil. The containers in the gardens discussed in this chapter range from 15–50 cm (6–20 in) in diameter. A bonsai dish is suitable, provided you do not leave it for long in hot weather, as a shallow dish with a small amount of soil will dry out faster in hot weather than a deeper one. A clean white polystyrene box as commonly used for fruit is a

Ledebouria violacea has silvery grey blotched leaves with deep plum reverses.

low-cost possibility if nothing else is available. Fill your container with soil or potting mix, and do not add fertiliser to begin with—you do not want your plants to grow big, just healthy!

When planning the planting of a miniature garden first define the viewing angle. If the container will be in the middle of a table, it needs to look good from all directions. If it is to have its back against a wall you will look at it straight on. You can create microclimates even in a tiny space. A taller plant, placed at the sunny end of a planting, will cast a shadow that will afford some shelter to the plants behind. If you want to grow sun-lovers, or if your balcony only gets a little sun, take care to position the largest plant so that it does *not* shade the other plants.

Miniature gardening is specialist country, and half

A bowl of sempervivums.

Seven tiny succulents in a pot 11 x 15 cm (4˜ x 6 in); the pink *Sedum* 'Aurora' grew too big.

Tiny *Sansevieria singularis* in a pot 12 cm (5 in) high.

the fun is discovering suitable plants, though you might not be able to find them at your local garden centre. Miniature plants do not appeal to many nurseries, as it costs as much to produce a tiny plant as a larger one, but it is hard to charge the same amount for them.

The best sources for miniature succulents are the mail-order catalogues advertised in the back of gardening magazines, and if you are not confident about your choice, the suppliers are always happy to advise and make up an assortment for you. Aloes, echeverias, haworthias, sedums, crassulas, aeoniums and even cotyledons all have miniature versions or very slow-growing ones, which for this purpose amount to the same thing. Add hardy non-succulent plants if you want, such as mosses, *Pratia*, *Cotula* and *Raoulia*. Alpines are good too, but take care to choose the hardier sorts that are scree dwellers. I do encourage you to experiment—in careful hands I have seen plants from the Arctic Circle grown next to ones from the tropics.

The leaves of some tiny bulbs can add interest to a planting and are useful as a foil for other plants. Crocus leaves, for instance, look like miniature reeds or flax. Some of the tiny cyclamen which come from around the Mediterranean are very hardy. Take care if you buy bulbs by mail order, though. The catalogues may describe tiny flowers, but rarely tell you the size of the bulb, and some tiny flowers have tiny bulbs, others have hefty bulbs. You do not want big bulbs taking up precious room in your container. I have grown the daffodil 'Tête à Tête', a tiny flower matched by a tiny bulb, in a fairly shallow bowl surrounded by *Echeveria* 'Violet Queen' and covered by a sedum. It survives and multiplies and adds seasonal interest to the pot. After flowering I tie the daffodil leaves into knots, so they continue growing and feeding the bulbs but look neat and interesting.

Adventurous souls could consider growing tiny succulent trees. A trunk has echoes of a grand cathedral, it is somehow magnificent, uplifting. A row of tiny trees makes an entrancing windowsill landscape, and they do not block out even as much light as a cyclamen. I have seen *Pseudobombax*, Money Tree or Guyana Chestnut, sold with plaited trunks and growing only to 50 cm (20 in). *Operculicaria* var. *decaryi* has small, dark bobbly leaflets which make an airy canopy. *Obetia radula* has a wedge-shaped trunk with a topknot of small fuzzy leaves, which can also sprout in little tufts all the way up its trunk. These are from Madagascar, Mexico, Brazil. *Brachychiton rupestris* is a neat Australian tree with a trunk that can swell with water. The juvenile leaves, dark velvety green with a fine white line down the centre, the mature

leaves light green and lobed, adorn the small crown lightly and can be kept pruned for a neat effect. There are several varieties, some with lobed leaves. This unusual and attractive tree is used as a street tree in dry regions, yet it can also thrive in a dwarf state. A friend showed me one that had been in the same 5 cm (2 in) pot for years—it had not increased in height, but neither had it died, so it is tough. I grow it in a pot. It is intriguing, unusual, and it gives me great enjoyment to watch experienced gardeners trying to 'place' it. The Bottle Tree, *Adansonia gregorii*, is another Australian tree which sucks up water in the occasional flood.

Grow these trees in such a way that even if they *wished* to get big they can't, that is, tiny pots, low fertiliser and meticulous attention to reasonably infrequent waterings. These are not succulents to neglect or to grow in places that become and stay hot. They like the same conditions as African violets— light dappled shade.

My sink garden, from bottom left: *Gasteria* 'Lilliput', *Echeveria minima*, *Sedum acre*, *Greenovia diplocycla*, a pink-flowering drosanthemum, *Sedum morganianum* and the stems of *Peperomia columella* just visible beside a variegated aeonium. The pink shaving-brush flowers of *Crassula teres* are centre front, next to a stone that directs the branches of a miniature acacia.

A sink garden

An old stone sink we replaced in the renovation of our kitchen made a charming miniature garden. I painted it with a stone-coloured enamel paint to make it look more garden friendly. I list the plants I used, partly because it will be some guide as to what is miniature and available (if you cannot find the exact plants you will be able to find exciting alternatives) but also to show how you have to be prepared to get plants everywhere you can think of. A garden such as this should be highly individual, there are no rules!

I chose the minute clustering *Gasteria bicolor* var. *liliputana*. A friend gave me some sprigs of *Crassula* 'Jade Necklace', whose leaves form rings around a fine wiry stem, giving the appearance of beads along the stalk. There are many crassulas with interesting shapes and fine leaves, which produce a froth of minute flowers like delicate meringue, often white. Just what I wanted. I dug up a piece of a tiny grey sedum from another part of the garden, and added the tiny *Aloe parvula*, gunmetal grey with a texture like sandpaper, and two little orthophytums, *O. vagens* and *O. saxicola*—both no bigger than my palm, whose finely toothed leaves looked like miniature agaves, one variegated, the other a soft caramel brown. 'Saxicola' means rock-loving, so I added some fine scoria to the earth when I planted this orthophytum, and just to be sure I also put one of my treasured rocks next to it to make it feel at home. Remember, a plant can like rocks either because they shade its roots or because it needs good drainage.

A small weed that looked like black lace suddenly appeared in one of my pots. Now, a weed is only a right plant in a wrong place, after all—it had a good, arresting profile and would add nicely to my horticultural 'textile'. Even a pedigree plant would be impressed with the 'attitude' of that small weed, I thought. I had a cactus shaped like a shiny green cushion with widely spaced spines, and also one that was small, white and fuzzy. I thought they might add a buzz, and would have the same effect as a neat topiary has in a garden. I scooped out a pocket in the potting mix and filled it with cactus mix for extra drainage for these two. I used the smallest echeveria—*E. minima*—in a pattern of five with macadamia nuts (baked in case they sprouted) placed like paving around them. A tiny *Peperomia columella* was irresistible—small vertical tubes with raised, boat-shaped lozenges along

Sedum mexicanum aurea and a variegated crassula tumble over *Crassula lycopodioides* and a crested sedum.

the stems. To soften the edges of the sink I planted the trailing *Sedum morganianum* and, new to me, *S.* 'Cascade' from a plant list (with a name like that, it just *has* to …) and, to soften a corner, the small trailing form of *Acacia pravissima*, the Ovens Valley Wattle, which tolerates periods of dryness. It will grow larger than I need, but it can be kept neat and trimmed.

A 'one of everything' garden can look a mess, whatever the size and whatever the plants used. To add structure I devised a grid from ice-cream sticks and planted it in a rhythmic chequerboard pattern of grey and green, then unified it all with a scatter of white quartz chips.

A tabletop garden by the sea

I was just about to throw out a yellow plastic bowl I'd found at the back of a cupboard, when I thought it might make a pretty miniature garden. It was 30 cm (12 in) in diameter, and I wanted to give height to the planting. The local hardware cut a length of white plastic drainpipe into three, and I found that a skewer heated on a gas ring would make a hole in the bowl and also in the bases of the tubes for drainage. Using masking tape to make stripes, I sprayed the tubes with yellow and pink aerosol paint, tied them together, and then weighed them down by half filling them with hydroponic clay balls for drainage (scoria would have done just as well). I used a well-draining mixture of cactus mix with compost and cow manure.

The bowl was a strong yellow, so I decided to use plants that had light, happy colours and wavy, swirling shapes that reminded me of the sea. In the tubes I planted the beautiful golden *Sedum mexicanum aurea*—a bit exuberant, but it can always be nipped back—a pretty green and white variegated crassula and, for contrast, *Agave stricta nana*, a small, stiff, golden agave only a little bigger than my fist. (I have an amusing pair of small pots shaped like heads and over the years I have had huge enjoyment in growing plants in them to give them 'hair'. The tiny agave had made one look punk and a haworthia as fine as grass had made the other look quite debonair—but a quick 'haircut' and both were liberated!) Around the base I planted a haworthia whose striped leaves seemed to writhe like the tentacles of an octopus, and took a sprig of a mid-green *Crassula lycopodioides* variety whose fine, stringy branches had something of the effect of a maritime pine. *Sedum lydium*, which looks like fresh green bobbles, foamed along the side and a crested form of *S. mexicanum*, a wavy, monstrous plant, was reminiscent of a clam-shell. *Ledebouria violacea*, with its fat bulb sitting on the surface and lovely, deep purple backs to its variegated leaves, added a bit of spice, as did a tiny *Opuntia* cactus which sat on the ground, small and interesting like spiky, flat tears, or yacht sails, according to your imagination. A sprig of variegated aeonium contrasted with a tiny geranium with very black leaves—an altogether satisfactory mix of colours and textures.

To underline the sea theme, I added a path of shells collected on beach walks (sprayed with lacquer to bring out the colours and add shine) leading to a bathing box (made from ice-cream sticks with much thought and much glue) and some modelling-clay seagulls.

Child's play

Succulents are ideal for children, for they are squash-proof, and even a tiny garden can have a rewarding mix of plants. Many years ago a small convalescing child piled earth into a bonsai dish so that one end had a hill. Holes were poked, and succulents collected from round the garden were pushed in and no harm done. We planted a small world. It had a path, and many stories. A twig of *Aeonium gomerense* made a splendid tree, bobbles of *Echeveria albicans* were either sheep or bushes. A stone made a ledge where there was something good, but the hole underneath it was lived in by 'bads'. Everyone *knows*, if you are three, that there are terrors at the bend of a path, so the path bent. Each time the story was different, but as we neared the bend the terror was real, and the summit was reached with a relief that was palpable. The small sister, meanwhile, had thumped her earth into an iron heap, and as we extracted the last squeezed hostage from small jealous fingers, and cuddled away the last tears of rage, I felt that if ever a little bit had been torn off from heaven and floated to earth it was that day.

A touch of whimsy to attract a child to gardening (or even a child at heart): a crazy, grinning frog with a punk hairstyle afforded by a miniature haworthia crouches at the feet of pots containing *Sedum lydium*, the tiny *Aeonium* 'Suncup', and a stressed *Sedum furfuraceum*.

Balconies and sunrooms

Gardening on a balcony or in a sunroom is the art of compromise. Such places can be windy or sizzle. But there is a plant for every place. Some nursery somewhere will have a plant that was found on a wild cliff that would thrive on your windy balcony, and something that sits and fries in a desert will just love your little oven.

A great many people have balconies which can be transformed by a careful selection of suitable succulents. On a windy balcony, a plant with wiry, flexible stems or feathery leaves is more windproof than one with paddle-like leaves. Asparagus have succulent cisterns on their roots which hold water; they are plants you can ignore for long periods, but the filmy foliage cannot be blown around. There are many compact but finely branched *Euphorbia milii* hybrids on the market which grow to about 20 cm (8 in), and which are almost never without cheery red or yellow bracts, if you find the original *E. milii* too large.

The floor-to-ceiling windows of a library filled with beautiful old books on the seventeenth floor of a high-rise apartment building look out onto a balcony measuring just 80 cm x 3 m (2 ft 6 in x 10 ft). The owner, Rodney Davidson, one of the founders of the Victorian National Trust, campaigned to preserve many of the historic buildings visible from his balcony. He is rightly proud of the view.

A Roman head forms a focal point for the succulents on this balcony. *Euphorbia milii* copes superbly at this windy height which faces the hot afternoon sun. It has 1 m (3 ft) long, loose branches. In winter it loses most of its leaves, but the bareness of the stems only emphasises the long, decorative spines that stud the length of each branch, and it retains a sprinkling of flowers (coloured bracts) most of the year. Selected for their contrasting leaf shapes and colours, several euphorbias, including a tall, white-streaked *E. grandicornis*, nestle up to the green tubular leaves of *Crassula* 'Gollum'. Hybrid and species echeverias and aeoniums all thrive.

Sunrooms have specific problems—no wind, but great heat in summer. Rodney's glass-enclosed sunroom, with a spectacular view of the sea over Melbourne's palm-lined Grand Prix course, is 'gardened' with *Euphorbia milii* and various *Schlumbergera* hybrids (Shrimp Plants or *Zygocactus*), which flower year after year and whose strappy, segmented leaves have become so large that one could accuse them of trying to listen in to the merest whisper of conversation. Their light green is set off by a particularly beautiful, fresh-looking geranium with dark, rich green leaves with lime markings, which reminds one that sometimes it is the attention to the smallest details that can lift the whole into something special. These plants cope in blazing sun, heat, and the absences of the owner.

Statuesque sansevierias are good on hot, shaded balconies and in air-conditioned interiors. Sansevierias come from the Congo, and tolerate low light, but not cold, so bring them inside for winter if the temperature drops below 10°C (50°F). If they get too cold they develop soft brown spots and can look as if they will die, but wait till spring, when they will almost certainly sprout again. Sansevieria leaves are often flat, like sword blades, and they have beautiful markings. They are in effect a sail, so are not suited for windy places where they can be blown about and snapped.

It seems to me that there is a great opening for a 'tiny plant place', a small nursery that would provide small plants and enough soil to fill a container, or a 'swappery', especially in areas where there are many apartment dwellers or senior citizens. It could also be a way to raise money for a charity. The 'makings' for a miniature garden would make a wonderful present.

7 Architectural Succulents

My top ten

Aeonium urbicum
Agave attenuata
Aloe barberae
Ceiba insignis
Cereus peruvianus 'monstrous form'
Dasylirion wheeleri
Furcraea bedinghausii
Kalanchoe beharensis
Opuntia species (cactus)
Yucca species
Companion bulb: *Albuca*

Succulents tend to have strong shapes and outlines that are very effective as part of a large planting. Most are long-lived, and over time can achieve a highly dramatic mass. If you want them to establish in an area where there may be long dry periods, water carefully in the first year or so after planting, allowing them to become fairly dry between waterings. This will encourage them to develop a good root system. Once they have developed good roots they will be reasonably self-sufficient.

Aeonium urbicum

Huge green 'roses' the size of dinner-plates make *A. urbicum* tremendously useful as a focal point. Winter-growing and with dramatic bright yellow flowers, the 'roses' hold their shape through summer if occasionally watered. (Aeoniums are dealt with at length in Chapter 3, Most Popular and Easily Grown).

Agave attenuata

Agave attenuata has broad, clean, prettily shaped leaves, and makes a compelling focal point. It can eventually grow a short trunk. The leaves are soft, and so it is a good choice if it is to be placed where anyone might brush up against it. Many agaves are spiky, with teeth along the edges of the leaves and a sharp spine at the end. Of course you can prune the spines, but a blunted agave looks pretty awful. Agaves are monocarpic, that is, they only flower once on a very old plant—some are called Century Plants because they flower so rarely. (There are a few exceptions, such as *A. bracteosa*, which are polycarpic.) Take great care when planting an agave, as some grow to an enormous size, weighing up to 2 tonnes, and become impossible to move.

Agaves and aloes are often confused, but both are superb accent plants with many varieties ranging from tiny to large. Agaves, furcraeas, dasylirions and yuccas (all closely related) from Central America, and the aloes from Africa, are all rosette plants, all tough, useful and beautiful. If you get impatient, even for a moment, hearing about 'yet another rosette plant', go and watch one in the rain, or play a hose on it, and see

A succulent vista in the Royal Botanic Gardens, Melbourne, *Agave attenuata* in the foreground against a flowering aloe.

A dramatic landscaping agave, possibly *A sisalana*.

how cleverly the arrangement of leaves directs water efficiently to the roots. Some agaves even shrink their trunks in dry times, leaving a gap in the soil, so that rain can run down and reach the roots directly.

Aloe barberae (syn. *A. bainesii*)

This is the largest of the aloes, from East Cape Province, a multiple-branched tree to 18 m (60 ft), with a rounded canopy. It has salmon flowers, and although it is said to be a forest dweller, I have seen it thriving in a suburban street, where it makes a delightful, unusual neat tree. It is fairly upright, and a tree that casts a fairly small shadow can be very useful in any garden. It is multiplied easily by cuttings (saw off a small branch).

Ceiba insignis

Many gardens need drama, and succulent trees are always glad to oblige. *C. insignis* is a small and prunable tree that makes a strong addition to a garden. It has spines shaped like sharp limpets on its bark,

probably developed to prevent wild animals rubbing up against it. Definitely not one to cuddle, it is extremely beautiful to look at, as the spines are just below eye-height.

Cereus peruvianus 'monstrous form'

To some degree succulents are a new palette of colours and shapes to play with, and their potential has not been explored fully in most Mediterranean landscapes that I have seen. If one is an addict of garden books, one only has to think of a box hedge to instantly imagine several dozen ways of using box. If one thinks of a 5 m (17 ft) high *Cereus peruvianus* 'monstrous form', it is likely that few precedents for using it will spring to mind. This cactus grows in tall columns, and is covered with bobbles, so that it looks … unexpected, is perhaps a kind way of putting it. I happen to think it is extremely beautiful. It will most likely be the only bobbly plant in the garden. It is the perfect contrast plant, and is particularly useful as it is a good, slightly glaucous green that other plants look good against.

Cereus peruvianus 'monstrous form' towering to 3 m (10 ft) against a setting of eucalypts in Jim Hall's garden.

It has soundproofing qualities, useful in town, and it grows as upright organ pipes so it takes up little room.

Dasylirion wheeleri

A very pretty, large puffball of fine grey-blue leaves up to 1.5 m (5 ft) high and wide from Arizona and New Mexico. The dasylirions, while slow-growing, are visually compelling as part of a mixed planting or as a focal point. They should be more widely used. The trunk can be split and used as cattle feed in dry times, and the leaves used as thatch or woven. There are smaller dasylirions available also.

Furcraea bedinghausii

A large flax-like plant, with a good silhouette. It will develop a stem, is tough, and eventually will produce the biggest, wobbliest flower spike it is possible to imagine.

A furcraea makes a dramatic outline against the sea.

Kalanchoe beharensis

This grows into a large plant, with great felted leaves, brown on top, grey-green underneath. It seems to particularly enjoy sandy light soils, but it is not fussy. Any little bit seems to grow. And it is powerfully beautiful. It would make a superb backdrop for a dark green cactus, perhaps.

Opuntia

Opuntias have dramatic outlines, flat paddles. They range from enormous to tiny. Opuntias available now are not the sort that went wild and caused problems by spreading very fast.

Yucca

There are many varieties of yucca, which send up massive spires of beautiful creamy white flowers at the end of winter. Related species include the dasylirions, furcraeas, manfredas and beaucarneas, which are all very hardy rosette plants varying in size from very large to small. They are all superb open-country focal points.

Companion bulb: *Albuca*

Southern Africa. 1 m (3 ft). Albucas build up into congested clumps which force themselves quite high out of the ground. Their flowers, white bells (*A. altissima*) or yellow bells (*A. canadensis*) hanging on a 1 m (3 ft) stalk, are similar to those of *Galtonia*. Galtonias are showier, but need better soil and have a shorter flowering season. Albucas are plant-and-forget bulbs and flower from spring to summer; en masse they are an impressive sight.

Many of the gardeners I mention in this book are men, and I should imagine that not one of them has pored over a coffee table book of dream gardens in other regions; perhaps as a consequence they have been free to pioneer new ways of creating beauty, sometimes when the odds are very long against them.

Both William Martin and Barry Rasmussen garden in the Mediterranean climates of southern Australia. They have baking sun and little shade. Neither supplements their meagre rainfall by watering, except for young plants, and then only until they become established. They both have a deep knowledge of the plants they use, and their plants thank them in the only way plants can—by looking content. On a hot summer's day, when everything including one's very soul is feeling a little dry, it is a quite extraordinary thrill to walk into a garden that glows all over with the *fun* of being alive. These two gardens are completely different in mood. There is nothing careless about their design, but they both have the wonderful quality of being carefree.

'Wigandia'

William Martin's garden is on the top of a tree-covered hill. The scoria that is used as a groundcover throughout this garden is the same colour as the rich red soil of the surrounding farmland. The scoria and *Echeveria secunda* are the unifying elements that not only tie the garden together internally, but also link it back into the vistas visible on every side. *E. secunda* is a small, 8 cm (3° in), hardy, clumping species which

Albuca in Jimmie Morrison's garden planted against a backdrop of olives.

In William Martin's garden solid topiary yews act as foils to an artichoke, some yuccas and a variety of succulents.

A vista framed by succulents in William Martin's garden.

laps the plantings like the waves on a beach. Sometimes it is placed singly, so that when it offsets it looks for all the world like green velour cow-pats against the scoria. (*E. secunda* can be mistaken for *Sempervivum* 'Hen and Chickens', but is much tougher. Never confuse the two when you are buying plants.) The flowers, on short stalks, are a long-lasting, pretty haze of pink and yellow nodding heads. In this garden the flower stalks are left to wither until they are black, when they are easy to remove with a slight pull. Meanwhile, the black stems set up a decorative, curiously dizzying optical buzz.

A snake-shaped bed filled with *E. secunda* divides the entrance path. The path up to the house begins with an asymmetric planting which includes a dramatic silvery artichoke. Nearer the house the planting develops a symmetry, achieved with pairs of agaves, aloes, cordylines and, unexpectedly, a pair of topiaried yews. The solidity of the yews sets off the strappy green leaves and towering creamy flowerheads of the yuccas.

Plants in this garden are used in bold confident blocks which emphasise the colours and shapes of their foliage. Stands of the giant *Aeonium urbicum* are planted in curves, cradling smaller plants, often smaller aeoniums. Blocks of agapanthus, strong and evergreen, look good in and out of flower. An enfilade of silvery grey *Cotyledon orbiculata* forms a guard of honour along a narrow path that leads to a raised garden, where the main living-room opens out on to a tiny lawn, the only part of the garden that is watered. This is designed, deliberately, as a tribute to the pioneering days when grass was necessary near the house to reduce dust, to prevent heat being reflected into it in hot weather and as a fire-retardant.

Abutilon hybrids (Chinese Lanterns) grow quite dense and slightly dwarfed in this dry garden. Feathery, unclipped rosemary frames a crisp *Agave attenuata* which is itself set off by green cotyledons. The strong outline of an aeonium floats again below the drying flowerheads of a deciduous sedum. An agave is placed, carefully, on the higher side of a path so that as its leaves open you can see the ghostly imprint of the 'claws' of the old leaves imprinted on the backs of the new, this beautiful diapering level with the eye to be easily seen and enjoyed.

Strong greens are carefully mixed with browns and greys, and this gardener has used only plants that revel in the sun, rather than defy it. A hugely knowledgeable plantsman, William enjoys plants as much for what they can *do* for him as for what they *are*, and nothing is included if it cannot cope with the climate. Gardens that have their roots in a cool climate can look sad at the height of summer—not his! Although this garden is tied in the bush with carefully placed vistas and looks very much at home against it, because of the strong personality created by the planting there is no mistaking that it is His Place, nor where His Place ends! A great gardener commented, 'This is the garden of the future', and one has to agree.

William has added greatly to the interest of his garden by making decorations out of zinc-covered corrugated iron. The entrance to the garden is flanked by Italianate pillars made from it. Seats, plant containers with supporting columns, all made from corrugated iron, form a powerfully unifying element in the overall design.

Barry Rasmussen garden

Barry Rasmussen's garden is quite different in mood. It also sits on a hill, but most of the native vegetation that once covered it is long gone, and the garden falls away to a grassy floodplain. In the distance, tall red river gums loom over untouched bush, their branches soaring like the ruins of an ancient cathedral. Rain here is infrequent but can be violent when it comes. The garden has fairly poor soil, but good drainage. It is full of mature specimens—succulents and Mediterranean plants—that have not only survived seven years of drought but also heavy frosts in winter.

Barry's success relies on an encyclopaedic knowledge of plants and their needs, and he finds most succulents can survive frosts—*providing* the drainage is good. Aloes and agaves are his particular love. His greenhouse, used to overwinter some of his most precious treasures, is made from polyflute which acts as both an insulator and a light diffuser.

The garden has a romantic feel; it is almost a hymn to the beloved plants. The beds are small and the paths wind comfortably, reminiscent of Victorian gardens, and this is done to best accommodate the huge number of unusual succulents and other plants he enjoys growing. This is a garden of *plants*, but—make no mistake about it—the garden is a joy because it is beautiful, not because it is a treasure-house of rare specimens. There are African, American,

A section of Barry Rasmussen's garden.

Mediterranean and Australian plants in the mix: the owner says you should 'make your plants work for you'. It is interesting that Barry and William Martin use this same phrase to describe their choice of plants, though they have not met each other. The only plants that sometimes look poorly in this garden are a drift of *Echeveria elegans* which, although they withstand the heat and the frost, do need the occasional watering over summer to look their beautiful best. However, they do not die, and are revived by the next rain, whenever it comes. The widely grown, beautiful, large *E.* 'Imbricata', 20 cm (8 in) across, its blue leaf with a pink edge, has naturalised in this garden, as has

E. derenbergii, a neat 4 cm (1° in) across. Barry says few of the succulents that seed germinate in the open—the seedlings are always to be found in the shade of a tree or rock, as they would be in the wild. A mature plant can be moved to full sun, but the small, vulnerable seedlings need shelter.

Aloes are a feature of this garden; they can become huge, so mostly are one of a kind plus the odd small spare. Two aloes, both from the Cape Province of South Africa, and both stemless, have great impact as garden plants. *Aloe striata*, 60 cm (24 in) across, has pale green, wide boat-shaped leaves with a fine pink edge; *A. buhrii*, which grows to 1 m (3 ft) across with

The orange spires of *Dykia rariflora* tower over its dark foliage in Barry Rasmussen's garden. The stubby, white-edged tips of *Agave victoria-reginae* are just visible in the foreground.

A bush view from Barry Rasmussen's garden.

H-shaped spots in longitudinal lines along the leaf has a reddish tinge to it and is profusely spotted under the leaf also. Although the leaves can suffer in an exceptional frost, they are otherwise very suited to Barry's conditions.

Barry uses dasylirions as focal points: they are beautiful and hugely architectural, with fine, spiky foliage, 1 m (3 ft) long, which radiates like a puffball. A mature specimen is a compelling sight. They can develop a small trunk with age and make an elegant contribution to a planting with their huge and dramatic flowers. Dasylirions are much grown in California. They are cold and humidity tolerant and will grow in poor soils, in sun or semi-shade. If you enjoy handicrafts, the leaves can be woven into mats or used as thatch. Propagation is by seed and cuttings. A dasylirion begins with grass-like leaves which develop decorative yellow 'teeth' along the sides. If possible place it where the sun will shine through them and light up the teeth like fairy lights. They are the Central American equivalent of the Australian grass tree (*Xanthorrhoea*), but do not have the long taproot which makes the grass tree so difficult to transplant. They are said to prefer heavy soils though they also thrive, here, in lighter soil.

Cheery clumps of green aeoniums, *Belamcanda* (Blackberry Lily), yellow kangaroo paws and scarlet crocosmias are set off by the soft grey of the grassy *Calibanus hookeri*, while *Yucca aloifolia* provides height. Lower down the hill an olive and a stand of

silvery-leaved *Senecio cineraria* tie the garden back into the soft greys of the landscape beyond. The whole mix is lightened by the reds of flowering aloes and scarlet gaillardias. Groundcover is provided by several varieties of *Lampranthus*, a little fat-leaved ice plant which is covered with brilliant pink and mauve flowers in spring.

Some interesting succulent hybrids are coming on to the market, often sold through supermarkets, and although a variegated aloe is reasonably frost hardy, a new variegated furcraea has proved problematic. A rare variegated *Aloe vera* is grown in a pot and carefully protected from the frost, but its next pup may not be so lucky because Barry can now afford to experiment. Because of the variety of plants and the fact that many succulents have flowers on long, hazy stalks, it was hard to photograph this beautiful garden successfully. Any breeze not only sets the flower spikes swaying, but also the many birds that are attracted to them foraging for nectar. Barry loves albucas, from southern Africa. They endure drought, and a great many varieties of them grow in superb clumps all over this hillside.

The overall effect of the foliage in this garden is of a *gentle* green—many of the plants are grey-green, softly striped or quietly edged, and as subtly coloured as the surrounding bush. There is a pervasive feeling of peace about the planting. The garden and the bush are well married—they seemed to be quietly content with each other.

Nichol garden

A curious feeling of silence pervades the succulent garden which surrounds Bill and Jean Nichol's house. It is quite incredibly beautiful. The spongy stems of the tall succulents seem to absorb noise; they are in fact green insulation. This garden has a strong personality. A towering stand of knobbly *Cereus peruvianus* 'monstrous form' looking like green organ pipes is nestled amongst prickly puffballs of *Aloe stricta* and bold-leaved agaves. It is accompanied by a plain *Cereus peruvianus* and both cacti are so tall—4–5 m (14–17 ft)—that their 'fingers' are outlined against the sky to great effect. The planting is a triumph, a superb example of the importance of texture in a garden.

Bill is a collector of plants. Six small greenhouses which are approached by a winding path are deliberately placed amongst the clever planting so that some are always hidden from view. One of the greenhouses is devoted to *Tillandsia*, another to *Conophytum*, with little glassy tops to their leaves—photosynthesis takes place deep down in these plants. *Dyckia* and strange cacti, beautifully variegated aeoniums, every part of the garden seems to be filled with a new curiosity. A slatted wooden roof erected to shelter tender plants from the full force of the sun has the effect of creating an outdoor room where a welcoming small table and chairs are surrounded by foliage.

'Bundaleer'

Matthew Brennan and Susan Spencer are professional gardeners whose garden 'Bundaleer' covers 2.5 hectares (6 acres) of hilly country. Though only partly surrounded by bush, summer fires are a concern here as only tank water is available. The house is protected from fire, icy winter winds and hot summer ones by a lush planting of deciduous trees, evergreen shrubs and groundcovers leaving a few distant, framed cameo views.

Their garden in divided into many small sections. Susan loves deciduous trees, roses, viburnums and buddleias, and her flowering shrubs drift and foam softly in the sheltered valleys where the soil dries out less quickly than on the hillsides. Matthew has cut elliptical rockeries out of the exposed, rocky hilltops where his succulents, especially his favourite sedums, thrive. The cold winds cause the sedums, crassulas and echeverias to put on their best stressed colourings. Never could you see redder crassulas, or bluer *Senecio mandraliscae*. The winter cold had turned the outer leaves of *Echeveria globulosa* an unusual mauve so

Various species cereus and *Cereus peruvianus* 'monstrous form', a variegated crassula, various agaves and aloes make a superb living wall in Bill Nichol's garden.

that its heart of tight grey bobbles looked like a pile of small iridescent pearls. *Sedum spathifolium purpureum* was a tight tumble of floury rosettes covered with white bloom, strung along shiny vivid red stems.　　*S. dasyphyllum* 'Lloyd Praeger', a prostrate groundcover, propagates in the wild vegetatively when heavy rains blast the small hirsute leaves off their stems and carries them away in runoff to re-root in new locations—at 'Bundaleer' the resident echidna, in its efforts to hunt ants in the rockery, manages to break off enough leaves to simulate the effect of heavy rain, thus helping to spread it throughout the rockery in a glorious drift. Echiums also thrive on the windy hills. Two dams add interesting views and microclimates. Susan planted an exquisite Bridal Veil Broom and prostrate grevilleas on the wall of one of the dams, while

Matthew had been so enraged by a long drought that he had planted hundreds of strands of the succulent *Carpobrotus edulis* around the other. Recent sudden rain and cold had stressed the carpobrotus to a scarlet colour and, covered with finely rayed magenta flowers, it floated hilariously when I saw it, like exotic water lilies, on the surface of the water.

Matthew also grows the carnivorous *Nepenthes* or pitcher plants; of tropical origin, they are housed in the garden's greenhouse. Some of the pitchers are as large as your hand and capable of catching small rodents. In the previous summer he estimated that between three of these plants over 2000 European wasps had been caught. *N. ventricosa* has some cold tolerance and is used as a parent species to breed hybrids with cold tolerance, but even so needs to be housed away from cold draughts and frosts over the worst months of winter.

Matthew Brennan's hillside of sedums in early spring.

8 Nurserymen, Hybridisers and Collectors

Each of the genera listed here has many beautiful varieties, and makes interesting collections. There is no 'best'. The best is what most appeals to you.

My top ten
Aeonium
Bromeliad family (includes *Bromelia*, *Dyckia*, *Aechmea*)
Cacti
Crassula
Caudiciform plants with swollen roots and stems (many species)
Echeveria
Euphorbia
Haworthia
Lithops (Stone Plants) and *Conophytum*
Sedum
Companion bulb: *Gloriosa rothschildiana*

The story behind the plants for sale in a nursery is stranger and more marvellous than one might suspect. A vast amount of material is grown by dedicated collectors who care passionately about the plants they grow. They are in effect the genetic 'bankers' of the plant world, and there is a close relationship between collectors and the specialist nurseries. The best nurserypeople not only sell you plants, they teach you how to use and hence to love them.

The age of the great plant hunters is not over, just quieter, and they are introducing new plants, and succulents in particular, that thrive in Mediterranean climatic conditions. They have even discovered rare new succulents in Australia. One recently found on a beach in Victoria is possibly a new species, and finding such a plant on a Portsea beach is rather like finding a new species on Coney Island or on the beach at St Tropez.

Sadly, plant rustling—the rapacious digging up of wild specimens to sell—remains a problem the world over. Unscrupulous plant hunters can wipe out commercially desirable species from a region. Certain echeverias have been eradicated from their Mexican habitats, as have august, ancient cacti from the deserts of the Central Americas. In South Africa it is the cycads that are under threat. In Australia the graceful tree fern *Dicksonia antarctica*, which can be easily removed from forests without its roots, and the grass tree *Xanthorrhoea resinosa*, with a long taproot that rarely survives transportation, have both been protected to ensure their survival. But responsibly done, the collecting of plants from the wild is sometimes their best chance of survival, when entire habitats such as rainforests have been destroyed. There are many more Golden Barrel cacti in cultivation than in the wild, for instance, where it is naturally restricted to a small area of central Mexico. Paradoxically,

Andrew Thompson with his tillandsias.

mining companies have been a great help to plant collectors worldwide since they build roads in remote areas that were once only accessible by donkey.

Nurserypeople, like collectors, have many different approaches. I was once in a shadehouse looking at a collection of succulents when I noticed a *Tillandsia streptophylla* whose silvery strap leaves swirled into an asymmetric swathe of tendrils. If I had been a composer I could have set it to music. Unaware there was anyone nearby, I said out loud, 'I think that is the most beautiful plant I have ever seen.' An unexpected voice quietly responded, 'I nearly killed myself getting that one, it was 10 metres up a tree.' It was Andrew Thompson, beard, ponytail, delightful smile, passionate plantsman, whose love of succulents has taken him all over the world searching for the rare and the unusual. He had found the tillandsia in Argentina, in a pocket of steep land between farming communities that remained uncleared. The local population is always glad to get money for a plant that to them has no

commercial value, but Andrew says it is always better to obtain seeds than plants, as plants grown from seed are more likely to thrive in alien conditions. He sells his plants at the Victoria Market in Melbourne, rather than having his own nursery, which gives him more time to spend with his plants. A vast number of customers support him where in the past perhaps one rich patron might have done so.

Another nurseryman, Lyle Filippe, believes that there are sufficient succulents commercially available in Australia already, and that what the average gardener needs is the confidence to use them with flair. The entrance to his nursery features a dramatic double row of the hybrid *Aloe arborescens* x *ferox*, a stunning sight when they flower in midwinter with huge, branched, red-orange spires. Lyle has travelled, but only to photograph how plants grow in the wild, and he has built a display garden at his nursery so that someone who knows nothing of succulents can instantly see them growing, and see that it is a different but beautiful look. He is always amused by people who say they don't like succulents, but after their first purchase come back the next week to buy more.

Some people prefer to get new plants by hybridising them. A hybrid is the progeny of a member of one race, variety, species or genus with a member of another. Wild plants have their own beauty, but a hybrid will have intermediate qualities between its two parents, and desirable qualities can be added or strengthened. Frillier leaves? More compact growth? Cold tolerance? You like it, but would prefer it in pink? The Japanese are said to discard 10 000 crosses to get one marketable plant. Hobbyists also produce hybrids, and they derive enormous satisfaction from the slow process of selection, saving the seed, planting, then waiting years to assess the full potential of their product.

For many years I had grown all the echeverias I could find, and I began to realise that most of my favourites—*E*. 'Alta May', 'Barbillion', 'Bittersweet', 'Chantilly', 'Dick Wright', 'Frosty', 'Lola', 'Mauna Loa', 'Pappy's Rose', 'Paul Bunyan', 'Silveron Red', 'Sundancer'—had been bred by someone named Dick Wright. I decided to track down the ones I did not have. Dick Wright had once lived in California, and on impulse one day I picked up the phone and, unbelievably, Enquiries put me straight through and Dick's jolly voice sounded down the line. I was as breathless as a teenager meeting the Rolling Stones.

Echeveria 'Blondie', a Dick Wright hybrid.

Echeveria 'Paul Bunyan', warty and wonderful, is a Dick Wright hybrid.

Dick and his hospitable wife Ruth live in a beautiful house on the edge of the upper Sonoran Desert. I was thrilled to meet the man whose plants had given me such pleasure for years. Everything Dick owned, including all his precious breeding stock, had been burnt to the ground in the 1982 California wildfires. He told me he had been so despondent that it was only after some years he began to buy back some of his hybrids and continue where he had left off. His life changed in other ways too. He bought a huge, shiny red fire engine and trained as a fireman and paramedic. Such devastation would never happen again to him or his neighbours if he could help it.

In the baffled light of his planthouse (his area is too hot for glass) I saw some beautiful new tiny aloe hybrids frosted with dots. But here were his echeverias, his lifetime's work, a venerable specimen of his early hybrid 'Mauna Loa', deliciously warty, standing next to its recent progeny 'Etna'. The volcanic inspiration for these names comes from the warty caruncles that erupt on the leaves of a mature plant of this breeding line. When aged and stressed, the caruncles turn scarlet/mauve/peach/purple. It is an extraordinary experience to stand looking at plants that have been conjured up by one man's dream.

We went to visit Renee O'Connell, a hybridiser working on a massive commercial scale. It was absorbing to see the two of them bent over her trays

of seedlings trying to estimate their potential, with Dick remembering the qualities of the wild plants he had begun with and Renee explaining how she had continued developing some of his lines and created

Dick Wright holding the hybrid echeveria which he named after himself. Photo courtesy Bev Spiller.

Renee O'Connell, left, with the author (centre) and a fellow collector. Renee hybridises echeverias and other succulents in California.

some of her own. Renee has bred some extraordinarily beautiful echeveria hybrids. 'Fractal' is one that will cause a sensation when it hits the market—the edges of the leaves are so frilly that they look like a fractal image—as will 'Blue Jay', and 'Truffles', a frou-frou of blue, frilly leaves that look as if they have been cut flat with a knife. Her attention to cleanliness is exemplary; ants are regularly sprayed, since it can be a disaster if a disease bug gets into a monoculture such as this. To me it was an eye-opening experience.

I had obtained a permit in advance from the Australian Quarantine Inspection Service (see Chapter 2, Acquiring and Propagating Succulents) in case I obtained any plants on my trip, so I was able to put my new treasures straight in the post and into the care of AQIS, while we continued on with our travels.

Not every gardener wants to have a garden as such, some preferring to build greenhouses or shadehouses for their plants. There are many advantages to be had in being able to see all your favourites at a glance, and being able to control all the variables—soil, water, heat and light. If plants are laid out neatly at waist level, it is easy to monitor them for signs of disaster or forthcoming flowers, and to harvest tiny seed capsules before infinitesimally small seeds disperse.

The world of plant collectors is fairly close-knit: who else but a fellow collector would understand the exact rarity of your treasure and be envious, or might know the whereabouts of an especially rare plant you have long wanted, or heard the rumour of a private sale?

It is always an absorbing experience to visit a plant collector and see the huge devotion and observation that goes into assembling and nursing a collection. Plant collectors seem to be able to grow *anything*. But Gordon Laidlaw, a famous grower and past president of the Australian Cactus and Succulent Society, says that understanding the optimum conditions for a particular plant can involve researching such variables as the season and amount of rainfall, or the precise rocks underlying the soil where it grows in the wild. Not surprisingly, a plant in cultivation can often attain a far larger and more impressive size than it ever would in the wild, where conditions might be variable and the enemies numerous.

Collectors are always on the lookout for freaks

A treasured cristate specimen. It is hard to tell that this was once a plain mammilaria cactus.

The hairy, undulating crested *Cleistocactus winteri* has great presence.

and aberrations ('sports'). It may just be luck if one arises, but it needs observation and skill to spot it and propagate it. Special care has to be taken with a crested plant—the complex shape can retain water and the plant can rot suddenly. In fact it is only by looking closely at such a plant that one realises how miraculously engineered most normal plants are to shed undesirable moisture.

Most collectors seem to enjoy putting together exhaustive collections of one species or genus, and having also a handful of rare, irresistible plants, and Gordon is no exception. It is always a magical

The extraordinary stem of *Othonna herrei* is not a malformation.

Haworthia with *Crassula* 'Hummel's Sunset'.

experience to look around. A pot of *Haworthia viscosa* can look as restless as a pot of propellers. The delicate, frosted wafers of *Titanopsis schwantesii* nestle into the soft gravel of its pot. A rare, prized *Othonna herrei*, the knobbly stem of which looks as if it had been made from a pour of quickly congealing toffee, with violet backs to its soft green leaves and tiny delicate yellow flowers. Intriguing and beautiful.

Dr Aleck Seltzer derives an intense pleasure from his two or three thousand haworthias. At a glance you can see just why such a collection exerts a strong fascination on its owner. The variety is endless. There are hairy haworthias, ones that glitter, some with shiny tops whose leaves reflex suddenly as if smeared back by a potter's thumb, others flat to the ground as if cut with a knife, stippled or striped. The arrangement on the waist-high horseshoe-shaped shelves is orderly, the pots all square, each plant set dead centre in its pot, and set off by pale quartz flakes. In most collections restricted space enforces its own discipline, and many collectors grow their plants hard, which means that they are small so that there is room for a vast number of different species. The space under the benches is filled with more, endlessly more, pots full of sansevierias and dormant or young plants. Two particularly lovely euphorbias look like cacti: *E. atrospina* has red spines which light up in sun, while *E. polygona* 'Snowflake' is powdery white, the spines along its ribbed sides bearing black fluffy blobs like the 'pills' on a woollen jumper. The effect against a white diffusing wall is eerily beautiful. An exquisite, nameless aloe from Swaziland with coloured lozenges running down its leaves looked so much like a precious textile that you automatically put out your hand to stroke it. An eau-de-nil *Kalanchoe beharensis* hybrid is appropriately named 'Velvet Touch' because the leaves feel like velvet. It is impossible to walk past some collections without marvelling at the magical plants that have been turned out by the Divine Computer.

In one of Aleck's glasshouses some lithops were standing 4–5 cm (1°–2 in) tall in their pots, a Herculean effort for any lithops, which are usually as earth-bound as a stone, no more than about 2 cm (∫ in) high. They had the same vermiculated top as a normal lithops, but also an extraordinary pale leathery underbelly, for all the world like a miniature breaching whale, or perhaps a giant molar. We went outside. The glum truth was so obvious that not a word was spoken. The neighbour had planted a cypress hedge

Lithops growing the way they should, in sun.

close to Aleck's fence, and had promised that he would keep it short, clipped. But cypress, planted 1 m (3 ft) apart, do not listen to good intentions, and the neighbour must have found it too hard to keep his promise. The hedge was cheerily shooting for the stars, and taking the sun with it. Aleck's plants needed more light than was now available. We stood in silence. A small but important tragedy was being enacted here. Sun is our birthright. Sadness comes in many forms, This was certainly one of them.

Companion bulb: *Gloriosa superba* 'Rothschildiana'

Tropical Africa. 1 m (3 ft). The scarlet and orange reflexed petals of flowers that somewhat resemble tiger lilies look festive over summer, and the soft green leaves of this plant are a very good foil for succulent foliage. Gloriosas have long stems which are supported by tendrils sprouting from the tips of their leaves. Grow in sandy soil, or in a large deep pot. The long, forked, fragile tubers bury themselves deep, and in a shallow pot will try and squeeze out of the holes in order to go deeper, and will often unhappily get stuck halfway. Leave undisturbed for many years. When the plant dies down in autumn lie the pot on its side at the back of a border, so that the bulbs stay bone dry over winter. In spring turn the pot up, put in place a tepee of bamboo and topdress with organic fertiliser. The gloriosas will climb through the surrounding plants.

9 Some Like It Hot

My top ten

Aloe plicatilis
Calibanus hookeri
Dudleya
Echeveria (grey species)
Hoodia gordonii
Kalanchoe marmorata
Nolina gracilis
Opuntia (Prickly Pear)
Pachyphytum oviferum
Sedum nussbaumerianum
Companion bulb: *Haemanthus coccineus*

Nearly all succulents cope well with extreme heat. As a rule of thumb, grey plants can withstand more sun than green, but there are exceptions to every rule. Hairy plants are usually tough, as are plants with hard, waxy leaves. Always be careful about planting a newly purchased plant of any kind directly out into the garden, as even the most sun-hardy plant can lose the ability to protect itself if it has been kept under a shady awning somewhere. It would be the same as if you or I went out into the full glare of the sun without a tan. Begin by putting it in broken shade, and over two to three days move it a little more into the sun until it takes the full sun. Small plants in the ground might need to be watered occasionally in the first year while they become established. My top ten seem to be particularly happy in full sun.

Aloe plicatilis

Western Cape Mountains, South Africa. To 5 m (17 ft). This is one of those extraordinary plants that has a limited distribution in the wild, but in cultivation seems to be adaptable and tough. In the ground the fan-shaped heads slowly build up and fork until it becomes the size of a small tree with a flat head. It looks majestic in bloom, with red tubular flowers, but its true beauty lies in its leaves. Grown in a pot it stays dwarfed. Mine is 40 cm (16 in) high in a 25 cm (10 in) pot after nine years. The strap-shaped leaves are arranged in two opposite rows, so that it looks like an open fan, and the shadows that one leaf makes upon

A trio that love sun: an unknown pachveria. *Pachyveria superbum* and *Pachyphytum oviferum.*

the next are particularly lovely. I place it so the morning sun shines sideways across it to maximise this effect, but it seems to grow naturally so that the 'flat' side of the fan is presented to the sun. *A.. plicatilis* does not seem to be affected by insects, so it always looks unblemished.

Calibanus hookeri

Mexican Desert. 60 cm (24 in). The only one in its genus, *Calibanus* has a dramatic caudex (swollen, succulent root), which sits halfway out of the soil, and graceful, grass-like fronds which grow from the top of the root in slightly punk-looking tufts. It is slow-growing but indestructible.

For many years I grew a calibanus in a hot and sunny conservatory. It grew happily in a small plastic takeaway food container (with holes punched in the bottom) which I had trimmed even smaller to fit into a strange but interesting stand. I used ordinary potting

Calibanus hookeri, the plant that lived in a baking conservatory—and loved it.

mix, but as the container was so small I repotted it each year. If it had been a child I would have been jailed for cruelty. After several years I planted it into a tall metal container which sits out in the full sun in all weathers, even the odd frost, and it has gradually built up. However, grown in the ground or given better cultivation the caudex can grow as large as a melon, and with dotty grass-like bunches sprouting out all over, it looks light and pretty.

In the ground the floppy mass of grass-like leaves has a soft silvery effect, something like a grass tree. It is smaller that most aloes or dasylirions, it is soft, and therefore good beside a path or where people can brush up against it. If it looks like grass why not grow grass instead? Because the caudex is most decorative, and definitely not grass-like, and *Calibanus* thrives where a grass would die. Also, it is fairly static: it will not suddenly get too big, it does not change as the seasons change, it does not need an annual trim, it never dies down. It would look wonderful grown as sentinels beside the drive in a hot seaside garden, or around a sunny pool. Plants that can survive in extreme conditions are often particularly useful in difficult spots.

Dudleya

USA, Mexico. Several varieties are available, 5–30 cm (2–8 in). Rosette or clumping, with pretty, silvery, fine leaves. Some are so heavily powdered that a drop of water on them will 'ball' and you will see a layer of talc-like powder on top of the water. Do not disturb the decorative powder by watering the leaves. Having said that, I grow several kinds out in the open in wind and rain and they still look terrific. Dudleyas are winter growers and send up spires of white flowers in spring. They are dormant but still beautiful during summer. Disconcertingly, they can shed most of their roots so that they become detached (in a strong wind for instance) but just place them back on the earth to re-root. In the wild dudleyas grow amongst rocks and seem happiest when on a slope.

Several varieties are available, including the elegant *D. brittonii* and *D. farinosa* (meaning 'floury'). They look something like an echeveria, but they store enough water in winter to enable them to survive through summer with no extra watering, which could be particularly useful if long absences are expected. They would pair well with *Calibanus* (see page 88). Some small, pretty hybrids are available which seem to be as tough as their parents. Dudleyas are beautiful in pots, but choose fairly shallow ones. Use a free-draining mix, 1 part good compost, 3 parts pumice. They enjoy it if the pot is tilted to mimic the drainage conditions of their habitat.

when the sun plays upon it. *E.* 'Emerald Ripple' has small, rich parsley-green rosettes which look fresh in the sun. Echeverias are beautiful when in flower. Remember that echeverias look best with more feeding and more water than most other succulents. Check for water every ten days in summer.

Superbly grown dudleyas.

Echeveria

Mexico. Grey species such as *E. elegans* and *E. secunda*, both 7–10 cm (2∫–4 in), tolerate heat. The grey *E. subrigida*, 20 cm (8 in), is especially lovely as a specimen, as its leaves are very thin and delicate with a faint pink flush which, together with the meal that covers them, makes them look luminous. The flowers are particularly beautiful because of the grace of the long stems. As flowering progresses the head slowly unfurls. Another grey one is 'Topsy Turvy', 15 cm (6 in), which has leaves that bend inwards like solid feathers. There are hairy echeverias such as *E. setosa* and *E.* 'Frosty', the softest fuzzy green, and the beautiful *E. pulvinata* 'Ruby', which has red-haired tips to its felted leaves and vivid scarlet flowers, adds great contrast in a mixed planting (surrounded by *E.* 'Gusto', for instance) and is one of those that shine

Echeveria 'Topsy Turvy'—great shape, great plant, but needs some water.

Hoodia gordonii

South Africa. With leafless, stubby, ribbed and spined upright stems to 40 cm (16 in) high, looking a little like a cactus, *H. gordonii* grows in places where the temperature soars past 50°C (122°F). The flowers are large in comparison, being saucer-shaped, brownish red and about 10 cm (4 in) across. This plant is used by the !Kung Bushmen to stifle hunger pains on long hunting trips, and is tipped to be the next slimming aid. Interesting to wonder if it could be farmed in Central Australia.

Kalanchoe marmorata

Eritrea. To 40 cm (16 in). A branching, sprawling plant with round, flat, green leaves which develop dramatic maroon blotches if grown in poor soil and full sun. Striking to look at, but you will need to occasionally neaten back the stems as they elongate. *K. thyrsifolia* ('Flapjacks') has even bigger leaves which grow flat against each other, and develop red margins in sun. Decorative, it mounds up into a subshrub.

Nolina gracilis

Mexico. To 3 m (10 ft) in the ground. The Ponytail Plant has a big, fat succulent root, a large part of which is visible above ground. Graceful, grassy leaves grow from the top like a ponytail. Fun and different, it makes a splendid specimen, but take care to surround it only with low plants so the great root can be appreciated. It also makes an impact as a container specimen. I bought one thirty years ago in a 5 cm (2 in) pot—it was potbound, and its taproot had grown like a corkscrew. Even after many years in larger pots and although other roots had grown, the taproot remained vestigial. However, this kept it fairly small, and it looks splendid, and healthy, in a plastic pot which fits inside an old chimney pot. The closely related *Beaucarnea recurvata*, the Ponytail Palm, grows in a similar way.

When you buy any tiny plant that is dependant on a taproot, and which you hope will grow large, ask the nursery if you can ease it out of its pot to check the roots to ensure it is not potbound. They will groan but it is worth it.

Opuntia

Southern USA, Argentina. 30 cm–3 m (12 in–10 ft) according to variety. Commonly known as Prickly

Kalanchoe thyrsifolia 'Flapjacks'.

Pear, opuntia cacti have flattened, rounded paddles which look particularly striking against the sky, and form a welcome textural addition to a low-water garden. Opuntias come in many sizes and shapes—oval, round and tear-shaped. The large ones can grow enormous, but are easily pruned with a chainsaw. The small ones, some with white spines, others with fuzzy yellow spines, make delightful 'pets'. The paddles sprout other paddles, and if you selectively remove them as they grow, you can end up with a 'Mickey Mouse' or a zigzag-looking adult. Some opuntias are smooth, but others have many spines and can look dramatic if planted so that the sun passes behind them. Opuntias can be green, variegated or grey. A pretty, unusual, medium-growing form for hot places is *O. gosseliniana* var. *santa-rita*, whose paddles are a soft violet when stressed. Any paddle will root. The fruit grows along the edges of the paddles. They turn red when ripe and are decorative and edible (slice the spines off carefully).

Nolinas can become huge and striking, like this one at the San Diego Zoo.

Pachyphytum oviferum

Mexico. 15 cm (6 in). Commonly known as Plover's Eggs or Sugared Almonds, *P. oviferum* has glistening blue-white, fat, round leaves, and pink and amethyst forms are occasionally available. The amethyst form is a slightly more robust grower, so leave space between them if you grow them together. The leaves cast beautiful shadows, and are at their best in full sun. Pachyphytums need good drainage; a grit or gravel and humus mix is ideal. They look good if left to heap up into a natural-looking pile, but they also make a very good, unusual edger growing over stones. Choose a place where the morning sun or a draught can dry off dew or rain. The flowers in spring are particularly beautiful, rather like small fritillaries, palest green with a cerise star in the middle. But they hang their heads, so if you wish to enjoy the flowers, place them high on a table, or find a tall planter so that the flower is at eye-level. Propagation is by removing an 'egg' (leaf), and placing it on its side in a pot; a plantlet will develop in about three weeks. This is another plant that will thrive with very little attention.

Pachyphytums have been hybridised with echeverias, giving rise to a group of plants named x *Pachyveria* which are attractive, drought tolerant and should be sought out. *Pachyveria* 'White Nun' is a crisp, fairly slow-growing, pale grey tumbler; 'Huth's Pink' is lolly pink; 'Supreme' is pink; 'Powder Puff' is a luminous blue-grey. All are thoroughly good garden plants.

Opuntia erinacea var. *ursina* has a great presence.

Sedum nussbaumerianum

Mexico. Grows to 75 cm (30 in) long over a couple of years. It retains its fat yellow leaves along the length of its stems so it is in effect a trailer. It takes full sun and grows easily from cuttings, though it is soil sensitive. I once put cuttings into two different soils and the resulting plant colours were quite different: one was the normal clear light yellow, the other an unhappy khaki. If by chance *S. nussbaumerianum* does not grow yellow in your garden, try moving it to another, preferably low-nutrient spot. Alternatively, it can be a yellow part of a parterre design. It mixes well with other colours such as the red jellybean sedums or blue *Senecio serpens*. The only attention this will need is to snap off the dead flower stalks after the starry white flowers die down in spring. *S.* 'Bert Stanwyk' is similar to *S. nussbaumerianum* but an olive green-khaki colour and good in full sun.

Companion bulb: *Haemanthus coccineus*

75 cm (30 in) across, and 20 cm (8 in) high. These strong, giant-leaved bulbs provide the best foil imaginable for the small-leaved and rosette plants so common amongst succulents. The flowers are interesting, but I grow this for its leaves, which are powerful, straight-sided and nearly oblong. Although *H. coccineus* loves full sun, the leaves become even larger if it is grown in the shade, up to 50 cm (20 in) long and 15 cm (6 in) across. Each bulb produces only two of these huge leaves, but the parent bulb is eventually surrounded by other bulbs, and it is then that they become truly spectacular. Imagine these strong leaves looping over each other, rather like a school of dolphins. I have seen people going to the trouble of tucking the leaves under to enhance this effect. If planted in the ground they spread to become a most striking groundcover. The leaves die down at the end of summer; I hide my potted ones until the flower, an amusing red shaving brush on a short stalk, emerges before the new leaves. The pollen on the end of each stamen is a bright clear yellow, so the flowers have a

joyful look. There are several varieties of *Haemanthus*, some fairly small and useful for the smaller garden.

The strange shaving-brush flowers of *Haemanthus coccineus*.

Huge haemanthus leaves made a good foil for various echeverias and aeoniums.

10 Shady Characters—and the Frost Tolerant

Many succulents prefer to grow in shade, in fact, they often grow larger and lusher in shade than in full sun. This should not be surprising because in the wild, where they use every possible technique to survive, seeds germinate more readily where the earth is dampest, and that is often on the sheltered or shady side of a bush or boulder, under or on a tree, the shadier side of a canyon. Succulents can survive in shade for part of or for the whole day. The imperative is, though, that the light be *bright.* Dank places in the shade are unsuitable. Fortunately, the light in a Mediterranean climate *is* bright.

My top ten succulents for growing in the shade include members of the bromeliad family, tillandsias and sempervivums—while these three are not precisely succulent, they have water-conserving characteristics. They have the same climatic preferences as succulents, but broaden the range: as rainforest plants the bromeliads and tillandsias enjoy heat, shade and also humidity, and the sempervivums survive well in cooler places.

So you have shade—what will grow?

Aeonium tabuliforme

Canary Islands. 10 cm (4 in) across, 1 cm (3/8 in) high. *A. tabuliforme* will grow in half sun, but it will heave a sigh of relief if you move it into the shade. In its natural habitat it grows in humid shade under trees or in the sea mists on damp cliffs. It is quite flat—it looks rather like a trilobite, but definitely alive! The overlapping, slightly hairy leaves look (and feel) soft, with a mesmerising symmetry, and it is impossible to pass by without giving it a pat. When *A. tabuliforme* flowers in its third year, you can lose it, but with luck it can leave small offsets to grow on. If you can bear to spoil the perfection of the overlapping leaves, a mature leaf (not taken from the outside where it will be old, or the centre where it will be too young) will strike. *A. tabuliforme* is an enchanter. Plant it in hollows between rocks; I have also seen it used with great effect flat on the trunk of a smooth-barked palm tree. It is one of the rare plants that enjoys growing on perpendicular surfaces.

Three aeoniums: *A.* 'Tricolour', *A. tabuliforme* and a variegated form.

Agave attenuata

Extremely restricted distribution in the wild—Jalisco, Mexico. 75 cm (30 in) wide, to 1 m (3 ft) high. This agave develops a short trunk in time, and is easily grown in sun or shade. You might not even have to buy one, because if any grow nearby you may be able to ask for one of the pups which are often produced around the base, and which can be detached easily. Ease it away carefully, even use secateurs, allow the cutting to dry for a day so it will not rot, and then plant it. *A. attenuata* is particularly beautiful—it looks clean, has a very sculptural shape and a lovely grey bloom on its leaves which is caused by a layer of fine protective powder. It is a quick grower, in the ground or in a pot, and if grown in deep shade will lean out towards the sun so that you can look deep into its cup. If it grows taller than you want, it is a simple matter to saw off the head, dry and replant. Like most agaves it takes a long time to flower, in this case about twenty years, but it makes up for it when thousands of flowers stud a stalk that can be up to 3.5 m (12 ft) tall, and which soars up and then bends over halfway up like an extraordinary inverted U.

One of the prettiest agaves is also easy to incorporate in a smaller, shady garden—*A. victoriae-reginae* is a neat grower, forming a most attractive round mound, the leaves edged with a decorative white stripe.

Aloe maculata

South-east Africa. The rosettes can be 30 cm (12 in) across. *Maculata* means 'blotched' or 'spotted', and refers to the decorative markings on the leaves. The flowers, which appear towards the end of winter, are a jolly red. This aloe is adaptable, growing naturally in many different habitats, and clumps up happily. It hybridises easily and there are several variants. It was used as soap by the Zulus. It is often seen naturalised beside the road, and is easily multiplied by the pups it produces.

I forget why I was dressed smartly, but we screamed to a stop anyway. I wrapped my arm in newspaper, put my hand under a stand of it with great care (it can be prickly) and got some pups for free … what *pleasure* that gives! It sits in a bush garden in a shady area with difficult clay soil, and has gradually grown into a solid thicket.

The red flowers of *Aloe maculata*, which grows as well in sun as in shade, are scattered amongst succulents including (centre) *Euphorbia pulvinata.*

Bromeliads

This large family from the South American rainforests includes dyckias, bilbergias and pineapples. 15–80 cm (6–32 in). Many members of the bromeliad family hold a dam of water in the central whorl of their leaves which traps and dissolves insects, and the nutrients so acquired feed the plant. Bromeliads like the same temperature range as succulents but they also enjoy damp air, so that a shady corner overshadowed by protective foliage suits them just fine. They will grow well in diffuse light and make long-lasting houseplants. Bromeliads have very beautiful, large flowers, often in shades of pink, purple, and vivid red and yellow. The inner leaves of many colour in an ornamental way, especially at flowering time. Be choosy when you buy, as they vary. The best are stunning. They like the same temperature range as succulents. Bilbergias survive anything. In spring they produce long, tasselled flowers on arching stems that are sugar pink, navy blue and vivid yellow. Extraordinary, compelling in the garden and sophisticated when picked.

A group of bromeliads with colourful leaves.

Cotyledon orbiculata

Cape Province, South Africa. To 40 cm (16 in). Described at length in Chapter 3, Most Popular and Easily Grown. The plain grey *C. orbiculata* var. *orbiculata* does well in shade, which is unusual as not many silver plants do well out of the sun. Cotyledons will grow in dry soil in dappled shade; give them a trowel of compost and a handful of fertiliser when first planting—they can probably be ignored after that. The green forms tolerate some shade, but will not flower enthusiastically. *C. orbiculata* var. *oblonga* 'Silver Waves', with its beautifully rippled silver leaves, grows lax in shade and will need cutting back more often than if it is grown in full sun, but it is still delightful. For people with small gardens *C. orbiculata* var. *oophylla* (egg-like leaves) is very pretty, slow-growing, and smaller, to 15 cm (6 in), its slightly hairy, pale grey leaves tipped with dark red.

Gasteria

Southern Africa. 5–40 cm (2–16 in). There are enormous numbers of gasterias available. In the wild they grow in the shade under trees. They have strap-like leaves, of various lengths, which look like tongues and often grow in the most striking configurations and can be striped, warty and shiny. Although some show

varieties benefit from being kept in a shadehouse to keep their foliage clean, most are splendid, unsheltered, in the open. They are also perfect in the difficult, rooty, semi-shade under trees, where they colonise to great effect. Warty gasterias are popularly called Mother-in-Law's Tongue. It is worth taking time to find one that really appeals to you, as they are very long lived. I have grown one for ten years in a soup tureen (I drilled a hole in it) shaped like a duck. It lives happily on a windowsill where it gets good light but no sun. Every three months or so I fill the sink with water and give it a good soak, then drain it until a newspaper

The gasteria in its modified soup tureen.

remains dry underneath it. Gasterias have pretty aloe-like flowers in spring, a spike of loose red bells hanging from a tall stalk. It is said they need good light to flower, but mine, on its shady sill, still manages to perform. In the open they like to be watered occasionally in summer, but will survive long absences by the gardener. Some offset slowly, and if they become overcrowded it is a simple matter to either pull off the smaller ones or dig them up, sort them out and replant.

Gasterias are shallow-rooted, so put some humus in the top layer of soil to help them settle. Once established they will survive on the sniff of an oily rag, as the old Australian saying goes. Planted beneath trees the branches will provide some protection from frost, although gasterias are reasonably frost hardy. They are very beautiful when grown well, and provide a perfect foil for both fine and solid-leafed succulents.

A few gasterias can be affected by a bacterial mould if subjected to cold temperatures. This manifests as a round, black patch of rot. Although disfiguring, it is usually confined to one or two leaves, and will soon grow out. The larger gasterias, to 40 cm (16 in), are more useful as garden plants, as the smaller varieties can be scratched up easily by birds (try a covering of chicken mesh if you wish to establish them in the ground). There are many exquisite, tiny gasterias from the size of a thumbnail to finger-sized which are perfect for miniature gardens.

This is Barry Rasmussen's list of gasterias for the shady garden. They are adaptable to various soil types, sandy to heavy, as long as drainage is perfect:

- *G. acinacifolia*: the largest, to 1 m (3 ft) across, a good feature plant; usually solitary leaves, very long and strappy in dense shade, stubbier in light shade; will also grow in full sun.
- *G. bicolor*: 50 cm (20 in), clumping, can be with or without stems; very attractive leaf markings.
- *G. batesiana*: 30 cm (12 in) clumps; rough, attractive light/deep green leaves.
- *G. carinata*: 50 cm (20 in), clumping; some forms have undulating leaves; var. *verrucosa* has white tubercles covering leaves, giving attractive appearance.
- *G. croucheri*: 60 cm (24 in), solitary or offsetting.
- *G. disticha*: 30 cm (12 in), leaves in two ranks, hence the name.

- *G. excelsa*: 75 cm (30 in), large; leaf margins sharp, usually solitary in habit; good feature plant, full sun also.
- *G. glomerata*: 20 cm (8 in), low-growing, densely clumping plant; unusual in having no leaf spots.
- *G. nitida*: 30 cm (12 in), solitary or clumping; will do well in full sun also; deeper roots than most.
- *G. pulchra*: 35 cm (14 in), elegant, upright, solitary or offsetting.

Haworthia

Southern Africa. Small rosette plants, mostly 4–10 cm (1°–4 in) across. Most like shade or semi-shade and like to be watered in summer, but kept drier in winter. Haworthias fall into two categories, hard and soft; the hard-leaved types are happy in sun or shade, the soft-leaved ones enjoy shade. I had a pot of a favourite soft-leaved *H. cymbiformis* in our porch for years. It had offset until the many plants crammed together formed a soft green dome. Everyone coming into the

A variety of haworthias thriving in a shady shrine.

house would pat it as if it were a dog. One day someone felt sorry for it and put it out to get some sun: it simply shrivelled. It was almost like a death in the family. If it had been accustomed to the sun more slowly it might have enjoyed the experience. Haworthias are neat and excellent for someone who likes exquisite, but small, plants. I am not alone in finding them addictive.

Sansevieria

Tropical Africa, India. To 60 cm (24 in). Sansevierias have upright leathery leaves and grow in the shady understorey of tropical forests. Their leaves are a good foil for rosette or fine-leaved succulents. You can ignore a sansevieria almost entirely if you need to—it needs only an occasional watering. Select by sight, if possible, as some have quite beautiful markings. There are many exciting new variegated clones. Some, such as *S.* 'Moonlight', a soft dove grey, are particularly stunning. Some are strongly margined. *S. trifasciata* 'Hahnii' is a fairly stumpy, easily available cultivar with yellow transverse bands on the strong green leaves.

Take a tip from their origins—sansevierias do not like cold, and can develop round spots of rot if allowed to get cold in winter, but as the weather warms they will grow new leaves and recover. They are superb in sheltered places in hot climates, and in conservatories everywhere else. They just love central heating, in other words they are good decorator plants for stairwells or offices. They can be ignored for many months, but do not forget to water them occasionally, and please, dust off the cobwebs.

Sempervivum arachnoideum

Europe. 3–5 cm (1˘–2 in). Sempervivums are rosette plants, often called Hen and Chickens because they offset and become surrounded by many small plants, forming attractive clumps. Sempervivums come from Europe, and do not thrive in the full sun of a Mediterranean climate. I have included them here because they are particularly useful for shady spots, and also for people whose climate verges on the unsuitable for succulents; they have a succulent effect without being true succulents. They are markedly less sun-tolerant than echeverias (with which they can be confused as they clump in a similar manner), but if left to increase naturally in shade, they will soon be surrounded by smaller rosettes, and the mats of small plantlets look attractive if allowed to tumble over an edge or a rock or nested into chinks between rocks or in a hollow log. They tolerate some sun as long as they are watered. I have grown the white *S. arachnoideum* for years in a gnarled, sun-bleached

Sansevierias are ideal for warm shade.

Always experiment; *Sempervivum achnoideum* was prettier in this mallee root than this *S. stansfieldii.*

mallee root (there happened to be a hole for drainage but I would have drilled one if there wasn't). As it grew, the root and the sempervivum melded together and it is now hard to tell where the root ends or the sempervivum begins. It is much admired. It is a simple process to renew when necessary—pull the clump apart, trim the roots, line the hole with flywire to keep the potting mix in, and replant.

S. arachnoideum is deservedly popular. It has fine hairs on its leaves, so that looks as if it is covered with spider webs. It grows well in shade and tolerates sun. There are many good red, brown and variegated varieties. Some spectacular new hybrids have large rosettes, about 20 cm (8 in) across, their fine hairs give them a romantic 'misty' bloom. They can be more temperamental than the smaller, traditional sempervivums, but this should not deter you from trying to grow them.

Tillandsia

Argentina and Brazil. 5–60 cm (2–24 in). Tillandsias are epiphytic, that is, they do not need soil, growing on trees or cliffs where the only source of water is occasional sea mists. Tillandsias absorb food and water through the fine scales covering their surface, which can be so large that they make the plant look as if it is covered with silvery hairs. The 'roots' absorb little food, being used almost entirely for anchorage. They like the same conditions—misted air and shade—as bromeliads, to which they are related, and they are particularly suited to the still, slightly humid air of shadehouses.

There are many varieties of tillandsias, silver, grey and green. Some have the appearance of celadon wool or finely curled paper, others look as if they have been carved from snow. The ones with thick and grey leaves tend to come from arid environments. The finer ones that look like thistle seeds come from exposed positions with higher rainfall, and the greener ones usually originate in shaded, damper forests. When you buy a tillandsia it is a good idea to give it an initial soak, as you don't know how long it has been in the nursery and how dry it is. A tillandsia leaf should look crisp and perky, not limp. Very weak fertiliser helps maximise their growth. Tillandsias are easy to grow and tolerant of some neglect. The danger is that you will forget to spray them in hot, dry periods—in which case they will die, but slowly, so you will be able to

Tillandsia sp. in flower

Tillandsia sp. in flower.

rescue them as long as you notice they need help. In very hot dry weather it is sensible to spray them every couple of days.

To mount a tillandsia, tie it to a support using the fine steel wire that florists use (copper wire is death) or a glue such as Gelgrip to attach the hard 'root' end to the backing. Cork bark, which is immune to bacteria and insects, a tree branch or even a door jamb make good backings. Ensure the glue has not formed a sump, and that the root can drain, because if a tillandsia 'root' sits in a puddle of water, it can rot. Also ensure you put glue on the root and not the leaf—as tillandsias slowly shed leaves from the bottom, if you glue them by the leaves they will sooner or later fall off. I use straw placemats (sprayed brown) and brushwood wreaths to mount them. Some people prefer to show their tillandsias against a dark background, but they would look wonderful at night if placed on driftwood on a dark wall and lit. Tillandsia flowers are surprisingly large for such ethereal-looking plants, often as large as your hand, and very beautiful—in vivid pinks and purples and yellows.

It is hard to say that one tillandsia is more beautiful than another. If you can get to a supplier to choose, select those that please you visually. Otherwise a good selection is *T. vicentina*, large, curly and grey; *T. magnusiana* for fine foliage; *T. caput-medusae*, exceptionally hardy, with tapering leaves that curl—it looks as if it has come from another planet; *T. harrisii*, neat like the top of a pineapple; *T. bitzii*, fine green, like curly grass.

Companion bulb: *Veltheimia*

Southern Africa. 40 cm (16 in). Excellent in shade or partial or full sun. Veltheimias have the most beautiful, glossy, evergreen leaves which are pest free. The flower appears as a pink spire in spring, rather like *Kniphofia*, and although good for cutting, if left will develop papery bracts which are highly decorative. The bracts are retained on the stalk for many weeks over the height of summer. (I have been known to spray them pretty colours for a party.) Each bract contains a large seed, which will germinate and quickly produce another bulb the same season. The bulbs, the size of a grapefruit, attractive, elephant-grey and pink and shiny, sit half out of the ground.

Once while replanting a clump I placed it in a pot and forgot it. It grew all summer in full sun and

The forgotten clump of veltheimias in flower.

Dramatic seed heads of veltheimias.

flowered and looked good, all with no soil. Tough. Veltheimias flower at exactly the same time in sun or in shade, which is very useful if you want to unify an area such as a courtyard where there is a variety of microclimates.

Barry Rasmussen (whose garden is discussed in Chapter 7, Architectural Succulents) has had thirty years' experience growing succulents. He has compiled lists of succulents that tolerate cold and frost which he has kindly allowed me to reproduce. Those who, like he does, garden in hot places that also suffer heavy frosts will find his suggestions invaluable. Opinions differ as to whether it is the formation of ice crystals that damages the cells of a plant or fast thawing in the morning sun. Some people swear that a pre-dawn hose reduces damage.

Barry's top ten succulents tolerate frosts to –4°C (24°F), and are chosen for ease of growth, visual appeal and availability. Remember that part of Barry's success is superb drainage, partly natural, partly devised—and that the frost resistance of many succulents increases with maturity.

Top ten frost-tolerators

Agave victoriae-reginae (Royal Agave)
Agave parryi
Aloe striatula
Cotyledon orbiculata var. *orbiculata*
Graptopetalum paraguayense (Ghost Plant, Mother of Pearl Plant)
Sedum rubrotinctum (Jellybean Plant)
Yucca australis (St Peter's Palm)
and three cacti:
Cereus peruvianus (Peruvian Apple)
Notocactus leninghausii (Golden Ball Cactus)
Trichocereus pasacana

These are not the only frost-hardy cacti and succulents, just Barry's top ten; he has listed another 35 that also tolerate frosts to –4°C (24°F):
Agave filifera
Agave parrasana
Agave utahensis
Aloe aristata (Torch Plant, Lace Aloe)
Aloe ferox (Cape Aloe)
Aloe polyphylla
Beaucarnia recurvata (Ponytail Palm)
Calibanus hookeri (see Chapter 10)
Cheiridopsis candidissima (Goat's Horns)
Cotyledon orbiculata

Dasylirion wheeleri (Desert Spoon)
Dyckia rariflora
Echeveria agavoides (Moulded Wax) cultivars
Echeveria elegans (Pearl Echeveria, Mexican Gem)
Echeveria 'Imbricata'
Echinopsis multiplex
Euphorbia resinifera
Furcraea bedinghausii
Hesperaloe parviflora
Hylotelephium seiboldii
Lampranthus coccineus (Red Vygie)
Mestoklema tuberosum
Pachyphytum compactum (Thick Plant)
Pachyphytum oviferum (Sugar Almond Plant, Moonstones; see Chapter 10)
Sedum pachyphyllum (Jellybean Plant, Many Fingers)
Sedum palmeri
Sedum spectabile
Sempervivum tectorum (House Leek, Hen and Chickens)
Yucca aloifolia (Spanish Bayonet, Spanish Dagger)
Yucca filamentosa (Adam's Needle, Adam's Thread)
Yucca gloriosa (Moundlily Yucca, Soft-tipped Yucca)
and four cacti:
Notocactus magnificus
Soehrensia bruchii (Golden Barrel of the Andes)*
*Trichocereus mandragona**
*Trichocereus spachianus**
*These three recently reclassified as *Echinopsis*.

Agaves will survive even heavier frosts, to –10°C (12°F). Barry's top ten agaves are:
A. americana ssp. *americana* 'Mediopicta Alba'
A. mitis var. *mitis*
A. ghiesbreghtii
A. guiengola
A. gypsophila
A. parrasana
A. parryi var. *huachucensis*
A. salmiana var. *ferox*
A. weberi
A. victoria-reginae

11 Succulents for Flowers

My top ten
Aloe ferox and hybrids
Cotyledon orbiculata
Crassula coccinea
Echeveria racemosa
Euphorbia milii
Hoya
Kalanchoe blossfeldiana hybrids
Portulaca
Stapelia and *Huernia*
Yucca recurvifolia
Companion bulb: *Crinum*

Aeonium urbicum in flower.

There is almost always something in flower in a succulent garden. Some of the plants in this chapter have been chosen because their flowers make a spectacular contribution, others because they are strange and fascinating. Some succulents have beautiful, long-lasting flowers, but with others, such as the euphorbias and some crassulas, it is actually the surrounding bracts that give pleasure. Bracts seem to remain at their peak for weeks, even months, far longer than the flowers themselves.

Aloes flower every year, some of the hybrids being particularly vigorous, their red and yellow spires providing a powerfully cheery note in midwinter. An agave, on the other hand, takes many years to flower, and all its energy goes into producing a single woody, towering flower spike, after which the plants dies, leaving plantlets around its base to replace itself.

The biggest flower spire of all belongs to one of the furcraeas, which was taken from the Central Americas to Mauritius and there, called Mauritius hemp, is a commercial fibre crop. Furcraeas are trunkless and slowly develop clumping, flat-leaved rosettes which could be mistaken for an aloe. The flower spike of *F. foetida* is spectacular, a loose candelabrum of small greenish white, highly perfumed

Lampranthus and drosanthemum in Barry Rasmussen's garden in spring.

flowers that can reach 8 m (25 ft). It is a very good container or courtyard plant. Conditions must have been just right for flowering, or perhaps furcraeas had been the fashionable 'must have' in nurseries one year, because a couple of years ago many of the gardens near mine looked as if there had been an alien invasion, the hilariously huge, unmistakeable and unmissable spires towering higher than the houses.

Some flowering succulents store energy in tubers under the ground, cleverly insulated from the worst of climates. They have a minimal amount of leaves exposed to the violent sun, but they are able to produce flowers out of all proportion to their apparent size. If you touch your thumb and forefinger into a loose O, it is about as big as the leaves of an *Orostachys erubescens* but it produces a 25 cm (10 in) spike of small yellow flowers, strong and large like a cat's tail, first horizontal then curling upwards, which lasts about three months. They offset quickly, so that the second year you can expect a positive *miauowery* of tails. Most satisfactory.

Shrimp Plants or Christmas Cacti, *Schlumbergera*

(syn. *Zygocactus*), are perennially popular trailers for hanging baskets, producing masses of flowers in early winter. Faucarias, with their little toothed leaves and shaggy yellow flowers, have a long flowering period. The ice plants *Lampranthus* and *Drosanthemum* provide sheets of colour in spring, many small flowers opening over their stems, while portulacas provide vivid flowers throughout summer. In California it is obligatory to plant such groundcovering succulents on slopes and house surrounds because of their fire-retardant qualities, a practice that might well be adopted in any Mediterranean climate garden surrounded by bushland.

There are curiosities amongst the flowers of the succulent world. *Umbilicus rupestris* (western and southern Europe), first mentioned by Dioscorides in the first century AD, has a cluster of completely circular succulent leaves similar to a nasturtium and, with the stalk centrally placed, looks like a toadstool. It is only 5 cm (2 in) high, but manages a hefty flower spike 30 cm (12 in) tall with a plume of yellow flowers. After flowering it dies back so completely it is hard to

Jimmie Morrison's welcoming garden. Note the small *Kalanchoe beharensis* to the left of the flowering aloe.

believe that a tuber remains hidden ready to sprout another year. Label such a plant carefully, leave it in a border over summer, and remember to watch for signs of growth in late autumn. This grows naturally in rocky walls in Europe; it is a most attractive curiosity.

Pachyveria superbum is an attractive rosette plant. When given to me it rejoiced in the name 'Super Bum' (*superbum* is the Latin for 'superb'). It is particularly beautiful, soft pink and smooth-leaved. The flower spikes develop slowly and are surrounded by an airy mass of bracts. One year it looked utterly beautiful. I decided to wait one more day before photographing it. There was a cataclysmic thunderstorm during the night—yet when I walked out the next day the wiry stems had bounced in the hail and it was untouched. It is a good pot plant.

If you expand the idea of 'flower' to mean 'colour', then succulents whose foliage colours brilliantly in winter or when stressed should be remembered. If you garden in dry country and really enjoy having something to mark the seasons, why not get colour from winter-colouring succulents, such as crassulas and echeverias, rather than deciduous trees?

Aloe ferox

South Africa, 1.5 m (5 ft). *A. ferox* and its hybrids have glorious rust-red spires of tubular flowers in mid to late winter, which is a wonderful time to have a cheery show. They have a stalk, sometimes branched like a candelabra, with kniphofia-like flowers. Aloes can be as big as trees (*A. barberae*) or small enough to fit in the palm of your hand (*A.* 'Dainty').

Cotyledon orbiculata

South Africa. To 50 cm (20 in). This group has been described in Chapter 3, but the flowers are so stunning that they cannot be left out of a list of flowering succulents. Remember there are two main forms—grey and green foliage—with pink-orange and red-orange flowers respectively.

Crassula coccinea

South Africa, South West Cape. 30 cm (12 in). Crassulas produce many small flowers that look brilliant in a mass rather than as individual blooms. *C. coccinea* is one of the best for flowers, although not a

A border of *Cotyledon orbiculata.*

very distinguished bush. It grows well by the sea. In early summer it produces the most vivid, deep blood-red corymb of tubular flowers. It does appreciate a little fertiliser because those flowers take a lot of energy to produce. I neglect mine shamefully in a seaside garden, but it still produces early summer fireworks. *C. perfoliata* var. *falcata* (syn. *C. falcata*), the Propeller Plant, has vivid red flowers and also an arresting habit of growth, the leaves twisting and radiating in a decorative manner.

Several crassulas have white flowers and brown bracts—nothing actually sets off a white flower as much as a dark surround—and the effect is like a large floral frogspawn. Such a plant, if set against the afternoon sun, lights up, and is unexpectedly beautiful. There are many tiny, columnar crassulas which tend to have flowers on long stalks held well above their foliage, and others, such as *C. teres*, with fine leaves that overlap like fish scales, their flowers, sprouting from the top, looking like a shaving brush.

Crassula coccinea makes a cheerful splash of red against flowering agapanthus.

Crassula cordata with its long-lasting flowers.

Echeveria

Central America. *Echeveria racemosa, E. pilosa, E. secunda, E. elegans, E.* 'Gusto', *E.* 'Mexican Giant', *E.* x *derosa* 'Worfield Wonder' all have really beautiful

flowers and are sold as flowering pot plants in many parts of the world. *E. racemosa*, with leaves the colour of brown sugar overlying dark green, has a flower spike with long-lasting red and yellow flowers borne in a neat head, fairly tall in relation to the plant. *E. secunda* and *E. elegans* are good in or out of flower. The yellow and orange flowers of 'Gusto' make a merry splash against its green leaves. 'Worfield Wonder' is lovely, but has to be fed to produce its best. *E. pilosa* hasn't got dramatic foliage but it does have a long, attractive flowering. *E. harmsii* has large orange flowers, but unfortunately few of them. The Inca used long-lasting echeveria flowers as offerings in their shrines Many of the beautiful hybrid echeverias have larger flower spires on long wobbly stems that last a long time when cut because the flowers continue to open after picking.

Euphorbia milii

Southern Africa, Madagascar. *Euphorbia milii* forms a bush up to 1 m (3 ft) high; the branches, themselves

Echeveria 'Gusto'.

The 'flowers' of *Euphorbia milii*.

Euphorbia milii.

Kalanchoe blossfeldiana hybrid.

1 m (3 ft) long, are studded along their length with foliage and long, greyish, decorative thorns, and seem never to be without 'flowers', which are in fact long-lasting bracts, the flowers themselves being insignificant. *E. milii* has vivid, pure red, fairly small but numerous 'flowers' all over the bush; its hybrids come in white, yellow, reds and pinks. *E.* 'Smoked Salmon' is a very pretty, small-flowering hybrid. A great deal of hybridising is going on, especially in Thailand, and large-flowered forms are becoming available. The hybrids are neater plants than the species, and with their strong, wiry twigs are perfect for windy balconies or smaller gardens, perfect for pots, wherever a touch of colour is appreciated.

Hoya

India, Asia, Australia. These succulent small vines are a connoisseur's plant. They have highly perfumed waxy umbels, often soft pink, scarlet or pure white. Beautiful new hybrids are available. They can be grown as lax vines or clipped, when the flowers will appear on the outside of the bush. They have neat, fairly sparse, succulent leaves and a long flowering season. Hoyas enjoy warm climates. Where there are cool winters, they need to be placed in sheltered corners.

Kalanchoe

Madagascar, Southern and East Africa. The *K. blossfeldiana* hybrids have especially pretty, bright and long-lasting flowers, one with fresh green leaves has a particularly vivid scarlet flower. *K. pumila* has grey leaves with lolly-pink flowers. Kalanchoes are easily struck from cuttings. The hybrid flowering varieties need good earth, or mix, to grow successfully. There are several attractive kinds with drooping bells good for baskets, which are sold under many local names.

Portulaca

Mexico, Australia. Flat mats to 10 cm (4 in). Hybrids with flowers in vivid shades of magenta, yellow and orange can be bought by the punnet, and make good bedding plants. Portulacas have succulent leaves and stems which radiate outwards. They love sun and benefit from a trim at the end of the season.

Stapelia and Huernia

Africa. To 30 cm (12 in). For those who like something decidedly different. Both genera are rosette plants with strange flowers shaped like starfish which are large for the size of the plant and often amazing shades of maroon and purple, sometimes deep enough to be nearly black. The flowers, often hairy, unfortunately

The extraordinary starfish flowers of a huernia.

smell like dead meat so are best planted downwind of those with sensitive noses. The stems of these plants are lax and leafless, and they rarely grow taller than 20 cm (8 in) but can form a mat with time. They are said to need a lot of light and heat to perform their best, but I have grown them outside without shelter and they have still flowered. They are curiously compelling and have a devoted following.

Yucca recurvifolia

Central America. 2 m (7 ft) high. This deservedly popular landscaping rosette plant is spectacular when it flowers in early winter, with spires of white bells. It occurs on sandy dunes and coastal plains but is tolerant of a wide range of conditions, and is frost tolerant. Propagate by seed or offsets.

Mixed succulents with a yucca in flower.

Companion bulb: *Crinum*

To 2 m (7 ft) tall in flower. Crinums come from tropical areas and are best in shade or semi-shade, though I have seen them growing well in sun. In my garden they do well in dry shade under camellia trees, where little else thrives, even though they are reputed to need damp conditions. Crinums have the most beautiful flowers, early through to late summer. They can be white or pink, cupped like a wine goblet (*C. moorei*), or with fine, thin petals that droop to great effect (*C. pedunculata*). Three or four flowers will be out on one stalk at any one time, and I have counted thirty buds on a head waiting to come out in succession. This makes for a very long-lasting flower spike. My sons once knocked off a 1.5 m (5 ft) stem with a football just as it was about to flower. I put it in a vase and went away for a month—it was still flowering magnificently on my return. Bulbs like this should be treasured.

Crinums provide a cool note in summer.

Be careful where you plant them, as the bulbs grow huge. They sit 30 cm (12 in) out of the soil and seemingly grow down for ever. Once established they are nearly impossible to move, and will spread slowly into a thicket. The leaves are green but it is hard to keep snails off them, so it can be sensible to put them towards the back of a planting. In early autumn cut off the leaves, and let fresh ones sprout. Be careful when cultivating around them as the flower stalk is produced from the side of the bulb, not the centre as in most bulbs, and it can be damaged.

12 Mod, Mad and Marvellous

My top ten

Aechmea recurvata
Alluaudia procera
Dioscorea elephantipes
Dyckia
Euphorbia grandicornis
Faucaria tuberculosa
Ficus retusa (Pot-bellied Fig)
Kalanchoe 'Fangs'
Monadenium ellenbeckii
Senecio articulatus
Companion bulb: *Massonia depressa*

Several succulent genera have varieties that are particularly extraordinary. Quite often it is the strangest attribute—a thorn, a root, a colour—that can have the greatest impact when carefully staged, especially in a domestic setting. Take care to highlight the drama inherent in a plant by placing it where it can be appreciated, and invent a background or a pot for it.

Aechmea recurvata

25 cm (10 in). A member of the bromeliad family. This elegant plant's shape is reminiscent of a pineapple. In spite of looking delicate, it enjoys sun or semi-shade. It has reflexed leaves which are designed in such a way that they create a cistern of water in its centre in which it traps insects for food, and which acts as a reservoir for dry times. Out of interest I measured the water I

Aechmea recurvata develops vivid leaves at flowering time.

tipped out of my aechmea—it pours like a jug—when it was 20 cm (8 in) high. It held two and a half cups.

For most of the year it is pale green, but in early spring the leaves turn a bright red and a bromeliad-like flowerhead emerges, vivid pink and purple. It is hard to imagine a more striking plant. I confess to fussing over it because it looks delicate, but a friend grows a cluster of them in her garden where they look like a huddle of fairy penguins about to set off for a walk. They never get any attention yet they spread and thrive. After flowering the plant slowly fails, but it will have produced a new pup or two to replace itself. Nurseries, however, mostly grow them from seed and they can vary.

Alluaudia procera

Madagascar. 3 m (10 ft) plus. An alluaudia is a long, thin, corrugated tube with spines along its length. It could be mistaken for a cactus. When growing well it has little leaves that stick out like jug-ears in decorative rows along its length. Although it is drought tolerant, if allowed to become too dry the leaves drop off (a water-saving measure) and the plant becomes dormant. Water it occasionally as the leaves are a great part of the attraction and it is a pity to lose them, though they grow back quickly once water is resumed. I am including an alluaudia in this list because it is amazing how often a tall thin plant can be a useful addition to a garden—to disguise an ugly downpipe, for instance. Somehow they have great personalities. People have been known to *talk* to their alluaudias!

Dioscorea elephantipes

Southern Africa. Root to 30 cm (12 in) diameter, vine to 2 m (7 ft). Dioscoreas are members of a large family that includes the yams, and they are grown for their ornamental, huge, cracked, corky root that looks as if it is covered by huge studs. Dioscoreas are ideal for pots. If planted in the ground, you need to be certain they have very good drainage, and will not be soaked by rain, as the caudex (root) can rot if wetted. In autumn it sends up a lax vine with pretty, fresh green leaves which needs support, but if unsupported becomes a good trailer. Take a tip from the way it grows: it seems obvious that dioscoreas in the wild must grow under something that will support the vine, which in turn is likely to shade the root. A burst of full sun on the root can burn it badly. It will survive but be scarred, so make

The magnificent root of *Dioscorea elephantipes*.

sure the root is sheltered from the sun.

When dormant, a dioscorea should be watered occasionally, as it has permanent little adventitious roots which sit waiting for the next rain. If kept totally dry the roots will wither and the new season's growth will be slower to begin. Watering should be resumed when the first sign of growth is seen (early spring). To encourage the root to grow large, repot every year when young, and feed with a very dilute fertiliser. When older it can remain undisturbed for years, growing as large as an oversize football and more. Propagation is by seed only. A dioscorea is filled with an edible starchy jelly that is said to be 97 per cent water. If it dies, only the outer shell will be left, light as a feather and highly ornamental, looking like a dormant tortoise.

To choose a dioscorea: these plants are sold when the caudex is about 8 cm (3 in) across. At this size you will be able to make out the beginnings of the cracks on the top of the root which will deepen into fissures. Choose one with large symmetrical pentagonal markings as these are the beginnings of the 'studs'. No two dioscoreas are the same, and although they are all beautiful, you will find that (as in a competition for the most beautiful baby) some undoubtedly have a 'wow' factor.

Dyckia

Brazil. 25 cm (10 in). A genus of small rosette plants whose leaves are notched, almost fretted, so that they look like snowflakes. Their colours range from vibrant shiny maroon to green and grey. They can be grown outside and make attractive edging plants. Very white dyckias are covered with a highly decorative meal and should be grown slightly sheltered or in a greenhouse, so that the meal is left as intact as possible. They would look superb lit with a spotlight in a small black-painted atrium, or in a planter painted scarlet and accompanied by a black aeonium or arum. Members of the bromeliad family from the Brazilian rainforests, dyckias need more water than most succulents.

Euphorbia grandicornis

South Africa. 1 m (3 ft). This succulent has superbly decorative, cactus-like, three-sided, free-standing stems. Some clones have beautiful, variegated growing marks and also prominent, decorative spines. It can

Dykia feseriana looks like a snowflake.

be kept inside for a while, as long as it is put out to 'breathe' occasionally. *E. trigona*, also cactus-like in form, survives humidity, and in the tropics can build up to 2 m (7 ft) high. Some varieties have very decorative maroon/purple markings in winter. Small, flappy 2 cm (∫ in) leaves stand out around the tops of the three- or four-sided stems. *E. trigona* will thrive in a sheltered spot in the average Mediterranean climate or a sunroom. Although reputed to survive low temperatures, the tips of mine died back after several sub-zero nights. No matter, the amputation of the dead bits sent it off to an alternate and multi-branched future, for if you shorten the stems, it will sprout more shoots.

Faucaria tuberculosa

South Africa. 5 cm (2 in). A small spreading carpeter with fleshy leaves which will flower whether kept in full sun or even light shade. It is ideal for a sunny position. Some faucarias have prominent teeth on the edges of the leaves and are sold under such names as 'Jaws' and 'Tiger's Jaws'. *F. tuberculosa* has protuberances on the top of the leaves as well as the teeth which makes it highly decorative, the tubercles being most prominent if it is under fertilised. When hungry it develops the most beautiful mauve bloom over its leaves—it needs to struggle. Feed it when young to encourage growth; once it has used up the fertiliser the carunculations will reappear, and on a much larger plant. Faucarias have shallow roots and need good drainage, so a handful of coarse sand should be added to the soil or potting mix. If you come across

A variegated *Euphorbia grandicornis* over 1 m (3 ft).

Faucaria tuberculosa produces intriguing flowers for many months.

have ever been to Angkor Wat you will have seen the strangler figs, whose roots have grown in and through the temples, lifting and separating the stones, and then grown over them, in effect forming a permanently enclosing web, as binding as any concrete … even if you have only seen photographs of them, you will forever realise the power of a plant with a caudex.

Pruning the feeder roots and repotting a *Ficus retusa* in the same pot for years has produced an impressive caudex.

an odd, shallow plantable container, think of *F. tuberculosa* as a candidate.

In summer it has cheery yellow flowers that look like shredded daisies. They open over several months punctually at 4 pm and close up overnight. Each flower opens for several days before dying. Decorative and tough, it might need repotting after a few years if it becomes too crowded. In the garden, it spreads into a decorative clump.

Ficus retusa

Asia. To 25 cm (10 in). The Pot-bellied Fig is a miniature ficus with fat, marvellously impressive, cantilevered roots. It will be content in a warm spot outside, but also makes the perfect house or conservatory specimen, becoming more beautiful as the years go by. Repot a little higher out of the soil each year to maximise the impact of the root. If you

Kalanchoe 'Fangs'

Madagascar. 1–1.5 m (3–5 ft). This is a striking cultivar of *K. beharensis* (see Chapter 6) with tough, felted leaves which are honey brown on top and grey underneath. It has prominent spikes on the underside of the leaves which give it an unnerving air—if it were human I think it would be a highly political animal. Unlike the species, 'Fangs' holds its leaves curving upwards, so that the spiky undersides are clearly visible. It looks particularly good if you are able to place it where the sun passes behind the leaves and illuminates the spikes which are themselves covered with tiny, shiny spines. Like all kalanchoes it needs

Kalanchoe 'Fangs'

Monadenium ellenbeckii.

good drainage, either in the ground or in a container. Very much one for a black leather and Doberman type of garden.

Monadenium ellenbeckii

Ethiopia. 25 cm (10 in). In the wild it can apparently build up to 1 m (3 ft), but mine remains small and tumbles neatly. It is composed of juicy-looking stalks, the leaves merely occasional stubs attached to the stem like flippers. *M. ellenbeckii* is pleasing because it is a particularly clear, pure green, and in winter it goes yellow at the tips. It needs free-draining soil. Monadeniums are not often grown, but I enjoy them greatly. Its larger relative, *M. coccineum*, 40 cm (16 in), is an upright plant (shorten it each year to prevent it becoming leggy), with a pale green stalk which stiffly holds out a few stalkless propeller-shaped leaves at right angles. It sprouts a couple of lobelia-like flowers from the top, little slippers of a powerfully

vibrant red, and they last on the plant for at least five months. It may not sound spectacular, and indeed it isn't, but its strong verticality is immensely useful in the garden. The famous pre-Impressionist artist, Corot, said a painting always needs a spot of red to focus the eye. If you cannot afford a Corot, plant *M. coccineum* instead, it has the same effect.

Senecio articulatus

South Africa. 25 cm (10 in). I have never met anyone who hasn't laughed when seeing this plant for the first time, and nothing is more important than laughter, in a garden or in life! *S. articulatus* is made up of vertical tubes about as thick as your finger. They look a bit like green sausages. During winter each sprouts a dear little topknot of soft green leaves, but the fun bit comes next. They grow another segment. So from looking like a sausage with a topknot it ends up looking like a string of sausages with topknots! It is said to reach 60 cm (24 in). It spreads by tubers which form an underground scaffolding, an anchoring system. It is shallow-rooted, and therefore useful for a shallow bowl. *S. articulatus* is good in the shade under a tree, and seems to tolerate sun. I have an idea that if kept moist all year it might retain the topknot, but it very much takes its chances in my garden and survives everything.

Companion bulb: *Massonia depressa*

South Africa. 3 cm (1ˇ in). Massonias are becoming deservedly popular. They have two stalkless leaves that lie flat on the ground like a fat figure of eight. The shape is very striking, and can be set off to advantage by a contrasting background, so they are a perfect choice for an offbeat gravel garden. Planted in a row they would look like dinosaur footprints. The flowers are fun, a bunch of small, straw-coloured or pink or white stars that sit low on the leaves like an old-fashioned shaving brush. There are many varieties available, but they are mainly propagated from seed and can be variable. Try to find a supplier who sells them in flower, when you have a chance to choose, although you grow this one for the long-lasting leaves and not the flower.

Drama—dream a little

If you want your garden to look different it is not only *what* you grow—*how* you stage your chosen plants is important. A wild and wonderful container, an extraordinary mulch, a vivid-coloured background can easily, sometimes cheaply, transform a space. You do not even need to be a gardener to get this one right, just a sense that things can be joyously different.

Imagine a wine-lover's patio, the plants mulched with corks. Perhaps even a baby cork tree mulched with corks. Or a photographer's courtyard, with plants rising from a tumble of white plastic film cylinders, some sprayed black, the odd one red. Choose a sculptural plant with a strong outline for this one, such as *Euphorbia trigona*. A mulch of Swarovski crystals might possibly be overdoing it a little—but only a little! Eco glass, a decorator item, is a good substitute. If you are going for a wildly unusual effect, it has to be immaculate. A mulch of beer-bottle caps looks amazing, provided it looks neat and deliberate, not just the contents of a waste can—no cigarette butts in this one. Make sure it looks as if you had the idea *before* that memorable party, and not after.

Old CDs work particularly well if they catch the sun at some stage of the day. They might set off white *Kalanchoe peltata* or *Cotyledon orbiculata*, or shine through a chunky forest of black *Aeonium arboreum* 'Zwartkop'. A row of Coca-Cola tins set at an angle like an old Victorian brick garden edging contrasts well with a froth of green parsley. (Vegetables sprayed gold look glitteringly rich for a special party.) A frequent traveller could use those annoying small foreign coins you always seem to end up with. I have seen pots decorated with mosaic made from broken china plates, in swirls of different colours; this effect can be particularly pretty if parts of a design such as flowers can be chipped off a plate. These are all low cost, high fun ideas, some of which may seem way over the top, but if you only have one small area, and if you just love to have the odd wild moment, and if you get bored with the same old thing, or if you just find a change therapeutic … then, why not!

Always be the judge of your own work; if you don't your friends soon will. Sometimes less is more, as far as impact goes. If you want to create a jungle, make sure that it is planned and planted with restraint, with attention paid to textures and mixes. Our lives can be so angst-ridden and busy that it is worth taking great care to make our surroundings a source of peaceful pleasure and content.

A tip here—if you put mulch straight onto the earth it can sink in and be lost. Agricultural weed cloth, cheap by the metre at any hardware store, will let water through and will keep the mulch on top. For a small area, or if your mulch is a pale colour, take a piece of white plastic, such as a heavy-gauge carrier-bag, and make tiny cuts all over to let water through. Place it over the earth and put the mulch over the top like the icing on a cake.

Pots and containers

Containers can be fun and give that individual touch to your patio or garden. A favourite pot will last forever and will suit many different plants over the years. Many, many years ago as a friend left my house she stopped by a particular succulent and couldn't help a snigger: 'You and your succulents …' I remember slowly walking back and staring down at that plant as if it was an unruly toddler. 'Well, *I* think you're beautiful, and I'm going to grow you so that *she* sees you are beautiful too.' I will never say a word against black plastic pots, they are the most useful things on earth. You can paint them, or place them inside a pretty pot or put them behind something else—but no two ways about it, a Beautiful Plant deserves to be set off by a Beautiful Pot. In my garden many a plastic pot has been hidden from view in little baskets bought at a charity shop, in 'nests' made from pruned vine tendrils, or wreaths of twisted fern leaves. A spray of aerosol varnish will prolong the life of these fragile beauties, although there is something very pleasing about the gentle decay of the natural world.

A superbpot is an investment and can be expensive, but great fun can be had by making your own containers out of odd objects. A masonry drill will put a drainage hole into *anything*, I have found—for instance, a pair of small soup tureens shaped like pigeons that didn't sell on a white elephant stall made a striking duo of planters with a hole drilled apiece. A chipped Japanese vase, a broken Vietnamese pot, a bronze Indian water-carrier, all drilled, made wonderful homes for succulents. The latter sat very flat on the ground so the hole was drilled low at one side, not in the bottom. I know a patio with a stand of old clay drainpipes of differing heights, no doubt discards from building sites, all upended, filled with earth and planted with tumbling sedums, crassulas, thyme and marjoram—it looks superb. Corrugated iron can be bent into many wonderful shapes, and even car tyres are a folk art form in certain places, fashioned into wonderful shapes.

Visit your local wood-lot and look for the weird hollow logs and odd-shaped roots that get piled up in a corner because they are hard to sell as firewood. Logs make superb containers; orchid fanciers vie for them. In some places it is illegal to remove hollow logs from the wild, as they provide shelter and nesting sites for wildlife, but if a tree is cut down for firewood from a designated area and subsequently found to be hollow, it is legal to sell it.

Some olive oils are sold in large and very beautiful tins. You might be lucky enough to have a neighbour who throws them out. These are not for everyone, but can give a young, funky look to a small patio. When you take the top off a tin, use the type of can-opener that leaves the rim intact so that the edges are strong and not sharp. A tin should be raised off the ground a little to slow down the rate of rusting; this will also prevent crawling insects getting in. Hardware shops sell grab nails, small galvanised plates with spikes on one side used to join two pieces of wood together. These come in various sizes, are very cheap, and I have found are ideal for raising small containers off the ground. You can buy decorative ceramic pot feet for larger pots.

You can plant any object that can drain if you line it with soft fibreglass flywire to keep in the soil (it can be bought by the metre). If you want to plug a large hole, say in a log, crumple up chicken wire or the tough plastic mesh which keeps leaves out of gutters,

Log planted with echeveria.

then put flywire on top to prevent the soil falling through.

The appearance of a container can be changed. Many people love the colour of rust, which can be achieved by rubbing a zinc container with salt. Sour milk or yoghurt (unpasteurised) can encourage lichen to grow on a concrete container or statue to make it look old; a spray of vinegar or bleach can remove green algae from stones. I buy small sampler-size paints in fits of enthusiasm to decorate pots.

Colour

Gardens in Mexico and the southern USA traditionally make wonderful use of colour, but some of us are shy of colour in the house and some of us are also shy of colour in the garden, which is even more of a pity. Colour is a tool that can be used with flair. If you enjoy the natural rhythms of the weather, choose limewash paints for your outside walls, as they deepen in colour when it rains. Impressionist painters saw shadows as violets or lilacs, and such colours seem to hum in the strong shadows of a Mediterranean climate.

Set against soft pumpkin, pots of soft-coloured terracotta or a vivid green or white would give three different looks, especially attractive if planted with fresh green plants. The soft, pale green fingers of

Sedum allantoides would look wonderful against pumpkin or aqua. Imagine an orange hibiscus against a bottle green wall, a hedge of artemisia, lavender, or grey *Cotyledon orbiculata* against lolly pink. Or a tiny area painted deep blueberry with fine 'snowflakes' of *Dyckia* or grey *Cotyledon orbiculata* against it. Black sets off grey plants superbly; even more chic, grey plants against a dappled grey wall. The soft starbursts of tillandsias look beautiful against any colour, but imagine a vibrant midnight blue for a contemporary look, or a soft grey-green for a romantic one. The scarlet bracts of *Euphorbia milii* would look wonderful against a sharp yellow or white, the bright purple leaves of the common *Tradescantia* against rose pink or warm pumpkin. The fresh green of *Crassula* 'Campfire' would look wonderful against any yellow, especially when it develops the vivid red colouring that it holds for months over winter.

I have a friend whose husband is a hard worker. He is said to leave his study occasionally for meals. However, she has been liberated in another way. They live in a 1930s house, the kind whose little bays and bumps make sense from the inside, but which can occasionally make for a slightly fractured look outside. I suspect he's never noticed that she has painted every single bit of the outside of their house every possible soft lolly-pastel colour. Not only is each flat surface a different colour, she has placed in front of each section a plant that is set off to perfection, so that a grand stand of grey cotyledon is set off by a singing quiet lilac, and when the soft pink flowers are out it is a sight that sends your eyes tingling with joy. She has a black *Alocasia* (Elephant's Ear), its great, black, shiny stems and leaves contrasted against a soft baby-blue wall. There is a huge, sparsely leaved tree by the driveway, and she painted on the drive in soft grey the shadow it casts at midday, so that even on a dull day it looks as if the sun is shining. The effect is joyous.

13 Designing with Succulents: Parterres and Patterns

Echeveria glauca, used here to form initials, offsets more slowly than *E. secunda*, so stays neater.

Bobbles of white *Mammilaria gracilis*, echeverias and graptoverias, including the pink *G..* 'Debbie', make a vase of flowers in this planter box which can be hung on a wall.

In this chapter I briefly outline different ideas for using succulents in original ways. A classic way of using plants is to treat them as *pixels*, dots, as design tools. In the nineteenth century municipal gardeners produced marvels of carpet bedding, making stunning use of flowering plants. In Mediterranean climate gardens it is possible to achieve the same effect using succulents as the building blocks.

Formal designs are for gardeners who are absorbed by the challenge of planning and *fiddling* with a project—the horticultural equivalent of embroidery. Consider using your initials; in the country, perhaps the brand you use on your stud horses or your sheep. For the minimalist, perhaps geometric stripes or concentric circles. A pattern of waves in a seaside garden, 'Tree of Life' designs—all these make good subjects. The design will last a season, even two, when it can be renewed by cuttings or by thinning out.

A small design can be planted on a wooden board to be hung on a wall like a picture. Secure potting mix to the board with mosquito netting, plant succulents through the holes and water. Such boards dry out

A design for a Christmas card based on *Echeveria secunda*, with *E.* 'Perle von Nurnburg' as the pot and *Graptoveria* 'Fanfare' as the star.

Suggestions for colour

White Cactus *Mammillaria gracilis*; *Echeveria elegans*, *E.* 'Lola'; *Cotyledon orbiculata*; *Dudleya farinosa*, *D. brittonii*; *Pachyphytum oviferum*

Blue *Senecio serpens*; *Dudleya* (blue form); *Kalanchoe fedtschenkoi* (large)

Green *Echeveria secunda*; *Sedum allantoides* (both pale green); *Echeveria* 'Emerald Ripple' (rich green)

Red *Echeveria* 'Tina' (small), *E. pulvinata* 'Ruby' (medium)

Pink *Graptoveria* 'Huth's Pink' (small), *G.* 'Debbie' (medium); *Echeveria* 'Perle von Nurnberg' (large)

Yellow *Sedum nussbaumerianum*; *Crassula* (variegated varieties); *Aeonium* 'Sunburst' (large)

Purple *Sedum spathulifolium purpureum*; *Graptoveria* 'Purple Dreams'; *Pachysedum* 'Ganzhou'; *Kalanchoe humilis* (medium)

Brown *Echeveria racemosa*, *E. nodulosa*, *E.* 'Butterscotch'; *Aloe* 'Hummel's Black'

Black *Aeonium* 'Zwartkop'; *Echeveria* 'Black Prince'; dark leaved gasterias and haworthias

Violet *Echeveria* 'Violet Queen' (small), *E.* 'Afterglow' (big)

Special effects

Neat blobs *Echeveria elegans*, *E. secunda* (both small), *E.* 'Lola' (medium); cacti

Carpeters Sedums, crassulas

Height Aeoniums, kalanchoes

easily but when well cared for make a pretty addition to a balcony or a courtyard. If you need succulents in quantity for this idea, plant the type you require in a well-drained, well-dug bed, add a little cow manure, and keep watered. It is amazing how quickly they will multiply.

Design plantings can be very effective in a tiny area such as a planter box in a patio. They are fun to create and need minimal maintenance. Three echeverias of a similar grey-green, but of different sizes, a topknot of the large *E.* 'Imbricata' perhaps, with an inner ring of the tiny *E. derenbergii* surrounded by an outer ring of the medium *E. secunda*, look subtle and enchanting when planted together.

To my knowledge the most interesting succulent parterres currently being created are at Waddesdon Manor in England, which was built by Baron Ferdinand de Rothschild in 1874. Today Waddesdon is a museum open to the public, keeping alive the tradition of grand gardens set by the first owner, who lived in the greatest and grandest part of the nineteenth century. Baron Ferdinand wanted the best, and that included the best in his garden. He would have seen miracles of carpet bedding. In an age when the windows and curtains of

Waddesdon Manor parterre: John Hubbard's carpet bedding design. © Clive Boursnell 2000.

the bedrooms were closed by servants at night, on special occasions the gardeners would work through the night by lantern, in order to surprise guests with a totally different planting when they looked out from their windows the next morning.

The current Lord Rothschild commissions artists such as Oscar de la Renta and John Hubbard to produce designs for the parterres. John Hubbard produced for the Millennium what was in effect a giant horticultural textile. A computer-generated programme devised by Kernock Park Plants, Cornwall, allowed the entire design of 70,000 variously coloured succulents to be planted in one day, and the result is an awe-inspiring sweep of vivid colour and texture.

Three-dimensional carpet bedding also features at Waddesdon, with steel planter frames on either side of the main entrance planted with succulents. For the Queen's Jubilee Year there were two huge floral crowns 2 m (7 ft) high. On the fiftieth anniversary of her coronation the crowns were repeated, but this time they sat on two ceremonial cushions. The jewels in

Floral crowns mainly composed of echeverias, Waddesdon Manor. © Hugh Palmer 2002.

119

At the end of a hot summer, these succulents are fresh and vibrantly green against scoria. Clockwise from centre front, *Sedum pachyphyllum*, *Crassula muscosa*, bronzy-green *Echeveria fasciculata*, two specimens of *Crassula* 'Hummel's Sunset' flanking *Aeonium* 'Zwartkop', the paddles of *Cotyledon macrantha* at back, *Banksia* 'Birthday Candles', a crassula in flower and a miniature aloe, front right—a satisfactory mix of plants.

the crown are large, showy hybrid echeverias and pachyverias. The garden teams planted the crowns on site using 70,300 plants for the two crowns and cushions alone. In 2003, for the 150th anniversary of Rothschild's Château Mouton-Rothschild wines, the parterres replicated the winery's first artist-designed wine label in succulents, complemented by two 2.5 m (8 ft) rampant rams, the family crest. Other years have seen giant doves on plinths. Creating these parterres and three-dimensional designs is all the more of a challenge because in England succulents have to be overwintered in greenhouses. Waddesdon's website www.waddesdon.org.uk is fun to visit.

My lawn was looking dreadful, but in the sixth year of a drought I could not bring myself to water it, so I decided to replace part of it with succulents. A visiting academic and famous gardener looked at an Aboriginal painting and said, thoughtfully, 'What a garden that would make …' That was it! Red scoria, to echo the red centre of Australia, and soft gold gravel would set off the plants I wanted to use.

I dug up a 4 x 6 m (14 x 20 ft) section of my lawn, which gave me an oblong with a north-south axis. I purchased a load of compost to improve the sandy soil, spread sterilised chicken poo, and covered the lot with permeable black weed cloth to prevent the gravels sinking in and stifle the weeds. Many succulents are stoloniferous, spreading by little runners, so a nice *big* hole for each one was needed.

I incorporated a great variety of succulents into the planting, which gives me more pleasure than using swathes of the same plant. Do I wish I was more disciplined? Perhaps. For the grouping that faced the sun I chose mainly grey and pale-coloured types, with pink, violet and lilac shadows, so the sun would shine *on* and reflect *off* them. A *Kalanchoe beharensis* I had grown in a pot for years had developed a particularly pleasing sinuous stem that defined a corner. Three oak-leaved kalanchoes along one side for height;

This is the rondel, the symbol for a waterhole, its shattered windscreen glass 'water' surrounded by rings of *Echeveria elegans* and *E. secunda* with *E.* 'Lola' (innermost ring).

some glitteringly white *Dudleya brittonii* like spiky footballs, a succulent plectranthus, grey with lovely violet shadows in winter, various forms of *Pachyphytum oviferum,* which billow like a miniature shrubbery, and sedums and crassulas to form drifts unifying the taller plants. *Aeonium* 'Zwartkop' formed a perfect foil for the soft burst of two puyas in front, and *Echeveria* 'Afterglow,' large with a soft violet bloom, added a bit of spice to the mix.

At the end which had its back to the sun, I planted green and brown succulents with red shadows, which light up when the sun shines from behind them. Green cotyledons; *Echeveria fasciculata*—bronzy-green with scarlet shadows along the ends of its leaves; the variegated *Aeonium* 'Suncup' (which forms a bush, and should not be confused with 'Sunburst' which has a single stem). I added a banksia and a black kangaroo paw for patriotic reasons; several 'Hummel's Black' aloes which are small and dark; *Crassula* 'Hummel's Sunset', green with vivid yellow and red tips. It will need nipping to keep it small. Succulents are forgiving; you can dig them up and move them around, and this encourages experimentation. If I made mistakes I knew I could correct them.

The centre was taken over by a rondel, the Aboriginal symbol for a waterhole or a gathering place, and three crescents which represent three people sitting around it. These were made from echeverias: *E. elegans, E. secunda, E.* 'Lola', amongst others. My neighbour's car had been vandalised. He was soooo grateful when I kindly shot out with a pan and brush to help him clear up the smashed windscreen glass. Little did he realise that I was plotting the Finishing Touch! I took to carrying the pan and brush and leaping from the car to collect smashed windscreen glass little by little wherever I saw it on the road. It was intended to create the quiet, deep effect of cool waters, and car windows are a softer colour than the bags of decorator glass that would have made the job simpler. My rondel was now a waterhole! I would love to think that in the quiet of the night I might wake from sleep and hear soft laughter below, that the ghosts of the original inhabitants of my hillside might happily sit, knowing that they were made welcome.

Except for some of the echeverias, which can need attention a little more frequently, I do not expect that I will need to water more than three times a summer, and then only to keep it looking fresher than it might otherwise do.

And has my conversion been a success? Let us allow the infant lily-pruner of the Introduction to have the last word. He invited twenty friends over to watch the world rugby finals, not knowing his brother had done the same. As the exhilarating game came to a close, inevitably a spontaneous rugby match broke out … over my succulents!

Succulents are resilient. Once a few corpses had been carried off and a few pieces replanted, apart from a spectacularly propeller-shaped *Crassula perfoliata* var. *falcata* that would never again inspire an aviator, and the lissom *Kalanchoe beharensis* that would be a goal post only in the great soccer ground in the sky,

the garden was smiling again. Every little bit that had been knocked off and missed the tidy-up seemed to take root, but a quick weed and the plantings were as neat as ever. I have come to the conclusion that gardens happen *in spite* of life and not because of it!

This book has been about listening to the Earth and trying to hear what it has to say. Call it 'Good Earth' gardening, perhaps—the Earth *is* good (it also happens to be the only one we've got), and if you make an effort to grow plants in harmony with both it and the climate around, it seems to appreciate your attempts to listen, to give powerful approval. Succulents thrive and look superb in Mediterranean climates which have extremes of heat and cold, prolonged dry seasons and often difficult soils. If you walk into the gardens in this book where the climate and the plants are well balanced, you might be forgiven for feeling that the Earth goddess, Gaia herself, is looking over your shoulder...and smiling.

Two tough trailers: *Pachyveria* 'White Nun' and *Graptoveria* 'Bert Swanwick' will add a graceful note to pots or rockeries.

Further Reading

Carruthers, L. and Ginns, R. 1971. *Echeverias: A Guide to Cultivation and Identification*, Bartholomew, Edinburgh

Cave, Y. 2002. *Succulents for the Contemporary Garden*, Random House, NZ; Florilegium, Australia.

Hamer, S.A. 1999. *Lithops*, BCSS, London.

Innes, C. and Glass, C. 1991. *The Illustrated Encyclopaedia of Cacti*, Quarto, London.

Irish, M. and Irish, G. 2000. *Agaves, Yuccas and Related Plants*, Timber Press, Portland (Oregon).

Kapitany, A. and Schulz, R. 2000. *Succulents for the Garden*, Schulz, Teesdale (Victoria)

Kapitany, A. and Schulz, R. 2002. *Succulent Success in the Garden*, Schulz, Teesdale (Victoria)

Rowley, G. 1997. *A History of Succulent Plants*, Strawberry, California.

Rowley, G. 2003. *Crassula: A Grower's Guide*, Cactus & Co, California.

Sajeva, M. and Costanzo, M. 1994. *Succulents: The Illustrated Dictionary*, Cassell, London.

Sajeva, M. and Costanzo, M. 2000. *Succulents II: The New Illustrated Dictionary*, Timber Press, Portland (Oregon).

Schulz, R. *Aeoniums* (in press, 2004).

Schulz, R. and Kapitany, A. 2001. *More Succulents for the Garden*, Schulz, Teesdale (Victoria)

Schulz, R. and Kapitany, A. 2003. *Succulents: Care and Health*, Schulz, Teesdale (Victoria)

Schuster, D. 1990. *What Cactus is That?*, Pierson & Co, Sydney.

Walther, E. 1972. *Echeveria*, California Academy of Science, San Francisco.

Wright, Ruth 1996. 'Dick Wright and his echeverias', *Cactus & Succulent Journal*, Vol. 68.

van Wyk, B. and Smith, G. 1996 *Guide to the Aloes of South Africa*, Briza, Pretoria.

Index

pulvinata 'Ruby' 90, 118
purpusorum 43, 118
racemosa 43, 106, 118
'Rosea Grande' 43
secunda 42, 43, **46**, 75, 89, 100, 106, **118**,
121
setosa 90
'Silveron Red' 82
'Sundancer' 82
subsessilis 42
subrigida 89
'Tina' 118
'Topsy Turvy' 24, **89**
unknown species **23**
'Worfield Wonder' **24**, 106
'Violet Queen' 64, 118
'Zorro' 29
Echinocactus grusonii 38
Euphorbia atrospina 86
bergeri 8
caput-medusae 32, 43
cuttings 33, 44
grandicornis 43, 68, 110, **111**
grandidens 43
heptagona 43
milii 44, 67, 68, **106**, **107**, 116
obesa 43
polygona 'Snowflake' 86
pulcherrima 44
pulvinata **15**, **95**
trigona 39, 43, 111, 114

Faucaria tuberculosa 111, **112**
fertilisers 20
Ferraria crispa 58
Ficus retusa **112**
Fockea edulis **18**
frost 25
frost-tolerant succulents 101
Furcraea 69, 102
bedinghausii 72
foetida 102

Gasteria 57, 96
bicolor var. *liliputana* 62, 66
frost-tolerant 96
shade-tolerant 97
Gloriosa 'Rothschildiana' 86

Golden Ball Cactus 38
Graptopetalum paraguayense 22, 44, 64
Graptoveria 'Bert Swanwick' **122**
'Debbie' 44, 50, **117**, 118
'Fanfare' 44, **118**
'Huth's Pink' 118
'Margaret Reppin' 44
'Purple Dreams' 118
'White Nun' 44
greenhouses 24
Greenovia 38
diplocycla **65**
grooming 29
growing hard 14
growing soft 15

Haemanthus coccineus **92**
hail 26
Haworthia 44, 57, **67**, **85**, **97**
cymbiformis 97
Hoodia gordonii 90
Hoya 107
Huernia **107**
Huperzia nummularifolia **58**

importing 35
insect control plants 27, 80
Internet catalogues 35

Kalanchoe beharensis 17, 44, 45, 72, 86, 120
blossfeldiana 44, **107**
cuttings **33**
delagoensis (syn. *tubiflora*) 45
'Fangs' 45, 112, **113**
humilis 118
fedtschenkoi **45**, 47, 50, 118
marmorata 50, 90
peltata **45**, 47, 50
pumila 44
thyrsifolia 'Flapjacks' **41**, 45, **56**, **90**
'Velvet Touch' 86

labelling 29
Lampranthus 77, 103
Lithops 63, **86**
fertilisers for 21
Ledebouria violacea 59, 60, **63**, 67